NOT FOR RESALE

FIXIN'S

by Jess Ritter

Illustrated by Wendy Wheeler

A CALIFORNIA LIVING BOOK

To Merle and Paul,
a mother and father wise in the ways
of rivers, hills and growing things.

And to Cynthia,
who gently insisted
that each word be right.

Portions of this material, in different form, have appeared in the author's columns and stories in the *Kansas City Star and Times, Outside Magazine,* and in the *Funfinder* magazine of the *San Rafael* (Calif.) *Independent Journal.*

First Edition

Copyright ©1979 California Living Books, The San Francisco Examiner Division of The Hearst Corporation, Suite 223, The Hearst Building, Third and Market Streets, San Francisco, California 94103.

Design/Production by David Charlsen.

Printed in the United States of America.

Library of Congress Catalog Card Number 79-51143

ISBN 0-89395-023-8

Contents

INTRODUCTION

Where I grew up as a farm boy, "running the hills" was a ritual part of growing up. It was that free time, when the corn was laid by or the potatoes dug, the hay put up or the fall slaughtering and meat curing done, when the child, boy or girl, was allowed to run free, to fish, hunt, gather hickory and hazelnuts, find woodchuck dens with an eager fyce dog, or just paddle a leaky boat across a river slough. I have tried in *Fixin's* to recapture the feeling of running the hills in a society that increasingly yearns for the touch of changing seasons, for the bountiful hills and hollows in the child's corner of all our hearts.

Born with an innate indoors-restlessness, I have spent a good part of my life working, fishing, hunting and gardening in the outdoors of California, Oregon, Washington and Idaho. The food lore here comes from such diverse sources as solitary Basque sheepherders in the Blue Mountains east of Pendleton, Oregon; Makah salmon fishermen in Neah Bay, Washington; logging crew cooks in the dense Douglas fir forests along the upper Rogue River; and, of course, the farm folk of California and the Missouri hill country where I grew up.

Fixin's, then, is a picturebook and storybook of good food and drink, setting down the bold imagination and lived gusto of Americans creating a new cuisine in a new and bounteous land. It is an invitation and a guide to rediscovering the tastes and gifts of nature that were enjoyed by almost everyone before the advent of convenience foods. It is not a polemic for the outdoor life, or for any of the natural foods diets that have become popular in recent years, or for a back-to-the-country movement. It is intended to show that even in an urban or suburban setting it is possible to sense that rootedness in the earth which comes from sensitivity to the changing seasons and to the growth of things around us.

The recipes and instructions for gathering, planting, making and preserving to be found in this book follow the cycle of the seasons. The food lore, stories, poems and drawings reflect that still-vital part of America where "doing it ourselves" is more than Yankee frugality — it puts us in direct touch with the rich, ineluctable earth-rhythms of birth, growth, fruition and regeneration.

Jess Ritter

SPRING

Planting Instructions

"Plant your corn
when white oak leaves
are big as a squirrel's ear."

     Said in the Oregon hills —
Oak rooted the families
Oak grained and oak sure
to slow maturity.

     Oak scarlet hillsides
and slow mule circling sorghum mill
promise Winter's sleep.

     Then green the increase of Spring,
the dreams planted deep and strong.

When Bodies Bloom

We Depression-children of the rural San Fernando Valley north of Los Angeles didn't measure time by clocks or calendars. We knew that spring was coming (and it was kite-flying time) when warmer days turned the Santa Susanna Mountain slope yellow and purple with blooming wild mustard. As days lengthened and there was enough light for a round of catch after supper, we knew it would soon be time to go to the ocean, to Castle Rock. Summer would be filled with marbles and tops, and then pomegranates. Still later there would be walnut pilfering, and we'd come home from school with hands ineradicably stained by the green hulls. It was fall again.

As adults, it is sometimes all too easy to let the seasons slip by unnoticed. The fresh perceptions of youth fade, and the years may tend to be marked only by the addition of one more birthday. Yet the rhythms of the earth's turning can reach us wherever we are. In crowded cities, where at night the stars are dimmed by lights and haze, I have been stopped on a spring morning by a pink burst of early flowering quince in a park, or a brave multicolored splash of early crocus poking through the detritus of a vacant lot. Today, from my study window, I look into the mazed white bloom of two gnarled Ben Davis apple trees in my neighbor's yard. The simple mystery of the apple blossom — snowy white with the faint desire of pale pink — is one of those perennial images of spring that we carry in our blood, just as the trees themselves carry the secret of the blossoming. Forty years ago those trees outside my window were apple switches brought to the Napa Valley from Indiana. In midwinter, dark and twisted, they sometimes look as barren and life-blasted as survivors of a battlefield. In spring, however, the unfailing cottony blossoms shout life into our corner of the neighborhood, and the accurately fumbling bees, dusted with pollen, respond.

Spring abounds with such joys. Ask any gardener who has just laid in his early-spring peas and lettuce; ask a gatherer of wild greens or mushrooms who has just returned from a day of foraging in fields and woods. They have found a way of pruning back boredom, depression, cynicism and despair, which to them are merely human graftings onto the eternal unfolding of miraculous births, necessary deaths and inevitable regeneration.

Gathering

Wild Greens

In California and the coastal regions of Oregon and Washington, the harbinger of early spring on the table is a bowl of fresh, delicate wild greens, dressed for a salad or gently simmered with salt pork or hamhock. The life-giving winter rains produce greens as early as February in the warmer southern regions, and the woods-wise forager, continuing the tradition of generations of coastal Indians, can continue to gather succulent wild greens until the June dry season sets in.

Far too many people have found themselves disappointed in their first wild greens experience. The reason for this may have been (1) the greens were too mature, therefore bitter, or (2) the dish was composed of *one* type of greens only, therefore limiting the range of taste. The larger the variety of greens in the pot, the better the taste, is a basic greens-gathering axiom. This also makes gathering easier, since several different varieties of greens are usually found growing together and tend to mature at the same time.

The six most plentiful wild greens in California and the Pacific Northwest are mustard (both yellow and purple), sour dock, lamb's quarter, deer's tongue, dandelion and miner's lettuce. These all may be found in practically every vacant lot, meadow and wood as well as on rural roadsides. Along the coast from San Diego to southern Oregon, wild New Zealand spinach grows in huge patches. Purslane and chickory, two greens of European origin, also grow in profusion throughout our area.

Most of the greens listed here contain more vitamin A than spinach; some contain more vitamin C than oranges.

There is one thing to watch out for: In the West Coast regions, greens such as sour dock, mustard and dandelion may winter over if there is no deep winter frost. These are dark green and *look* like they have toughed-out the cold weather. Avoid these and go for the lighter-green, smaller new growth. Much tastier.

The final gourmet touch to a wild greens dish can be made by adding wintered-over spinach or Swiss chard from the garden (in the warmer regions) or by adding the delicate, early-spring thinnings of these. If this is done, add the spinach and/or Swiss chard during the last few minutes of cooking.

Country Greens

Wash and pick over the greens, discarding woody stems and the inevitable grass. Place the greens in a large pot, cooking with the water that adheres from the washing. Add a piece of hamhock or salt pork or 2 tablespoons of diced bacon and simmer very gently for about 20 minutes. It's as elegantly simple as that. These greens fit naturally into a dinner of simmered ham and marrowfat or navy beans and Indian Cornbread (page 246), which may be used to sop up the nourishing "pot likker." Some folks slice open the cornbread and cover it with the beans or greens.

Smothered Greens

This is derived from a Northwest Indian recipe.

¼ cup diced bacon
3 green onions, tops and all
1 tablespoon honey or brown sugar
⅓ cup white vinegar
½ teaspoon salt
¼ teaspoon fresh ground pepper
2 to 3 quarts washed greens

Fry out the bacon in a heavy skillet until crisp and brown. Add the onions and sauté until soft, about 3 minutes. Stir in the vinegar, honey, salt and pepper; stir and heat for 5 minutes. Put the greens in a wooden salad bowl, pour over the hot dressing, toss and serve.

Wild Green Salad

Using the ingredients at hand, West Coast Indians and early settlers prepared many variations of this basic earth-borne salad. My country ancestors in the Midwest passed along a treasured dressing recipe for wild greens. My grandmother claimed her recipe derived from the Indians of the Piedmont area in Virginia. The forty-niners of the California gold rush used miner's lettuce and watercress for the chief greens supply. If available from clean water, the watercress imparts a nice bite to the flavor.

1 quart spinach, watercress, or miner's lettuce
½ cup sliced green onions
1 pint mixed wild greens
⅓ cup oil
¼ cup cider vinegar
2 tablespoons honey or brown sugar
1 teaspoon salt
¼ teaspoon fresh ground pepper

Mix the dressing ingredients in a jar and shake well. Mix greens and green onions in a wooden salad bowl and toss. Dress with the oil mixture and toss again gently.

Wild Mushrooms

Morels   Of the over two thousand edible mushrooms in the world, the elusive, reddish brown morel (*Morchella* species) is the most highly prized. Delicate yet meaty, light yet filling, the morel is the patrician of mushrooms, and the morel hunter is the dry-fly fisherman of mushroom hunting. Morel hunters, normally outgoing and friendly people, become taciturn, evasive and downright shifty-eyed when questioned about their sources of supply. They are often found in the woods disguised as birdwatchers or bee-followers. On discovering a single morel or a spreading clump a morel hunter first looks to see if he is being observed, then sidles up to his delicate prize, plucks it and swiftly stows it away.

Morel mushrooms are distributed throughout most of the United States, and the lucky gatherer may, in certain years, find them in profusion, usually in isolated groves of oak trees. I know European-trained chefs in Portland and Seattle who pay more than $25 a pound for morels imported from France, yet they grow annually right there in the forests of the Cascades and the Olympic Peninsula.

Morels are found in the spring in open woods and along streambanks. They reproduce in no discernible pattern. A bee-loud oak glade that one year produces a bushel of morels in a large patch may produce none, or only solitary clusters, in successive years. Morels vary from reddish brown to gray in color. They are stalked, pitted and have spongy rounded or conical heads (morels are often called "Christmas-tree mushrooms"). All species of *Morchella* are edible, but there is a poisonous *false morel* to be avoided. The caps of false morels are folded, brainlike, rather than spongy, and they are chestnut- to coffee-colored.

Morel mushrooms dry easily and may be reconstituted for cooking with scarcely any loss of flavor.

Besides the shy morel, there are eight other easily identifiable edible mushrooms common to California and the Pacific Northwest. *Caution:* No one should attempt to gather and eat wild mushrooms without instruction and explicit guidance from experts and without using a reliable four-color mushroom guide book. It is best to stay with the more easily identifiable species; stay completely away from the clearly defined and deadly species of *Amanitas.*

Meadow and Horse Mushrooms (Agaricus campestris and *A. arvensis)* Varieties of meadow mushrooms are grown commercially; they are the familiar button mushrooms found in cans on grocery shelves. They have purple brown spores (for a spore test, tap the mushroom over a sheet of white paper). Meadow and horse mushrooms grow in pastures, meadows and lawns throughout the United States and Europe. In Northern California and the coastal region of Oregon they are especially plentiful after warm winter and spring rains. The cap is dry and white in the button stage but becomes brown as the spores mature. Some are covered with brown scales. The gills of the meadow mushrooms are white in the small button stage, distinctively pink in the mature stage, turning chocolate brown as spores mature. The ring is prominent and delicate; stem and cap separate easily. The larger horse mushroom has a delicate anise odor and taste; gills, at first white, turn dark brown. The large hollow stem has a thick ring with the lower surface frequently split. Meadow and horse mushrooms are frequently found growing together, especially in Northern California.

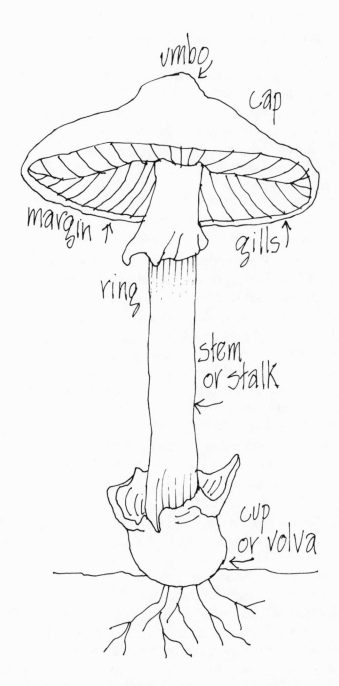

Orange Delight (Lactarius deliciosus)   Found in coniferous and hardwood forests in California and the Pacific Northwest, especially in the foothills of the Sierra and Cascades. The cap is zoned in shades of orange; gills and stems are orange to yellow. Greenish stains or blotches appear where plants are bruised. Wounds also turn green. "Milk" is reddish orange. No ring or volva. Some caps become funnel-shaped when mature, and zoned with concentric markings.

Oyster Mushroom (Pleurotus ostreatus)   In the woods of California, Oregon and Washington grow what native mushroom hunters call the chicken, garlic and oyster mushroom — each tasting exactly as the name suggests. The beautiful oyster mushroom also has an oysterlike white-to-gray color. It grows on logs, stumps and living trees. The fan-like clusters usually grow in ascending rows, clasping tightly to the wood and curling over at the outer edge of the cap. Oyster mushrooms toughen with age, so the new ones are quite the best. They especially like to grow on downed trees near clear streams and rivers.

Edible Bolete (Boletus edulis)   In France this is the famous cèpe mushroom; in Germany, it is the treasured Steinpilz. Unlike the other edible mushrooms of the West and Northwest listed here, the bolete has spores instead of gills on the underside of the cap. With the round toasted-bun appearance of the cap and thick pestle-shaped stem, the bolete is easily identifiable. They are especially compatible with spruce and rhododendron thickets, where they spring quickly into bulbous existence through dead leaves (and as quickly decay, for they are exceptionally juicy). The *lurid bolete* (aptly named!) is poisonous, but is easily identified. Shaped like the edible, it has, however, a bright-red to maroon pore surface. Also, a raised network of red lines, fair warning, covers the stem. The best test for a lurid bolete is the flesh, which turns blue when cut or bruised.

Chanterelle (Cantharellus cibarius)   The European market mushroom. Two varieties — the egg-yellow true chanterelle, which smells like an apricot, and the vermillion chanterelle, often abundant in California and the Pacific Northwest, which has a bright cap, gills and stem. Chanterelles are among the best mushrooms for drying.

Shaggymane (Coprinus comatus)   A distinctive, easily identifiable mushroom, abundant in the fall in meadows and woodland clearings in California and the Pacific Northwest. Shaggymane, and its edible cousins the inky caps, are black-spored fungi which eventually digest themselves in an inky fluid that develops in mature specimens — the entire cap may liquefy in a few hours. The oblong or cylindrical cap has scattered, fluffy or scruffy scales. Since shaggymanes do not dry or keep well, they are the true mushroom-hunter's mushroom, abundant will-o'-the-wisps that, lightly browned in butter, are a bright but quickly fading gastronomical dream. Amateur mycologist Tom Robbins, writing a few years ago in *Seattle* magazine, valiantly tried to define the flavor of shaggymane as "a slightly meaty taste combined with something like the perfume of burning leaves."

Puffballs (various genera)   All puffballs are edible when young, white and solid, and are the most easily identifiable of mushrooms. For most farm children, giant puffballs *(Calvatia gigantea),* which may get as large as ten pounds, exist chiefly for stomping, when the dried specimens *whoosh* out an impressive cloud of chocolate-brown spore dust. However, a logging camp cook from La Grande, Oregon, in the Blue Mountains, showed me what a delicacy giant and spiny puffballs *(Lycoperdon pedicellatum)* can be when sliced, dipped in beaten egg, rolled in cracker crumbs and sautéed. In Northern California, Washington, Oregon and Idaho, puffballs are generally found in the fall, after the rains. In the Sierra and Cascades, where there are summer thundershowers, July and August are also good puffball months. One giant puffball can easily feed a dozen people.

Preserving and Cooking Mushrooms

Morels, oyster mushrooms, chanterelles and orange delight mushrooms dry well. The best procedure is to spread them in a single layer on a cookie sheet and give them sun and more sun over a period of three to five days, bringing the trays in at night to avoid nighttime moisture. However, the best mushroom hunting season in California and the Pacific Northwest coastal areas is during the rainy late fall and winter months. During this time of year, thread the fresh mushrooms on a string, leaving enough stem to separate the caps (or thread "collars" of any dry material between each mushroom). Hang the strings of mushrooms in a warm dry room, preferably in a sunny window. They will shrivel, turn very dark and look plain ugly, but in those little wafers you will have the very essence of the woods, leaves and earth. Store the dried mushrooms in a tight jar in a cool dry place.

The use of dry mushrooms is limited only by your imagination. They may be reconstituted with water and sautéed; they may be thrown dry into stews and soups. They may be powdered and added to casseroles, soups and sauces. Perhaps the best drying mushroom of all, available in the Pacific Northwest, is the pine mushroom, or *matsutake,* as it is known to the Japanese. Pine mushrooms, an essential ingredient in sukiyaki, are frequently broad-shouldered giants that can measure ten inches across the cap. They are generally found in the fall.

Baked Mushrooms

A perfect dish for serving that surfeit of big, fat meadow or horse mushrooms often available by the bucketful in pastures after a warm fall or winter rain.

1 pound large mushrooms, wiped with a damp cloth
¼ cup butter
¾ teaspoon salt
¼ teaspoon fresh ground pepper
¼ cup fine bread crumbs
¼ cup chopped black olives, hazelnut or English walnut
    meats (optional)

Carefully remove the mushroom stems from the caps; slice the stems. Place the caps, hollow side up, in a flat casserole dish or round pie plate. Scatter the sliced stems around the caps. Melt the butter in a saucepan; add salt, pepper, bread crumbs and olives or nuts, if the latter are used. Carefully pour this mix into the hollow of each mushroom. Bake for 30 minutes in a 300° oven, basting the mushrooms a few times with the melted butter.

Planting the Spring Garden

The Answering Earth

A garden is not verbal, does not exist to be described, bragged about or complained about. There will be books to read, information to share with other gardeners, and discussions about this year's potato bugs or puny butternut squash, but much of what we know will come to us directly from the garden itself through our five senses, and be returned to the garden, wordlessly, in the way we care for it.

Its response, though still wordless, will be eloquent of sensual bliss: Watch the glorious evolution of a creamy, fluted, hibiscuslike okra blossom or fondle the smooth skin of a sun-warmed Big Boy or Big Girl tomato right off your own vine. Experiences like these have the power to draw us immediately close to "the force that through the green fuse drives the flower." During a lifetime of gardening I have relished and stored into memory many such moments.

While working my way through college and graduate school, I earned school money by working the summer pea harvests in eastern Oregon. On the high, nighttime-cool slopes of the Blue Mountains north and east of Pendleton, Oregon, and Walla Walla, Washington, grow some of the highest quality fresh peas in the world. During the pea harvest, from early June to the end of July, canneries in small towns like Weston and Milton-Freewater, Oregon, operate around the clock freezing and canning the succulent Oregon peas.

During the last two of these summers our family moved into an old farmhouse east of Milton-Freewater on the banks of the clear, noisy Walla Walla River, and I put in a garden while my wife and I worked twelve-hour shifts in the cannery.

Our fertile riverbank garden plot adjoined a similar one belonging to a long-time resident — a tall, thin black man of at least eighty who habitually wore clean, faded bib overalls and a pressed, collarless white shirt. We gardened literally side by side, exchanging at first only polite good morning nods, though I noticed him eyeing very closely my rows of green beans and tomatoes. Finally, one June day Mr. Robinson quietly and formally welcomed this squatter to the neighborhood by commenting favorably on my flourishing crop of Kentucky Wonder pole beans.

During the first hot spell of late June, we stood at the lot line sharpening hoes together, preparing to attack stout jimson weed and tangled purslane.

"I almost didn't garden this year," said Mr. Robinson, tucking his file into his hip pocket and carefully directing a brown stream of tobacco juice at a nearby preening grasshopper. "My wife died on me last October and I was black in my mind all winter. Didn't seem to want to do much of anything, except keep the stove full of firewood all winter. Me an' Mannie was married 61 years and it still don't seem right bein' out here in the garden withouten her washin' jars, gettin' ready to put up beans and pickles. But my mind's a lot lighter if I can keep it outside the house."

During that summer of twelve-hour shifts in the cannery and, later, night-long truck drives along dirt mountain roads with booming loads of freshly cut pea vines, Mr. Robinson set me on the road to a lifetime of bumper-crop potatoes. The old man taught me how to pick off the red larvae of the dreaded potato beetles and drop them into a tin can of kerosene — and how to mulch deeply the potato plants with grass, weeds, corncobs or straw.

With the ease of an old friendship, we jointly dug potatoes during one fiercely hot July afternoon. Mr. Robinson went into his house to fetch a stoppered jug of buttermilk, cooled by a wrapping of water-soaked burlap.

"My chil'ren tell me an ol' man like me's got no business achin' his back in a big garden, but I tell 'em my back'd lock up stiff as a bed-slat if I sat in a chair all day watchin' tv like a lot of old folks. Yep, me'n this garden'll be around for awhile."

He paused, offering me the jug of buttermilk, then gazed musingly for a bit into the middle-distance of the wide, dappled shade of the sycamores along the banks of the river. Driving the corncob stopper home into the buttermilk jug with a pop of his hand, he flashed a wry grin at me. "I just misdoubt endin' your life by sittin' around."

The Compleat Gardener

In the process of writing newspaper columns about gathering, gardening and preserving nature's bounty, I have met countless people hungry to garden but intimidated by what they think is the complexity of the task. Yet with proper tutelage and patient, close observation of the habits and nature of growing things, any novice can start a successful garden — even become a skilled gardener after only a couple of growing seasons. Best of all: At the minimum, it takes no more space than a sunny walkway and a strip of ground along the sidewalk, a few window boxes, or a half-dozen containers or large flower pots. Even an apartment-dweller with only a patio or balcony can grow a full summer supply of tomatoes, lettuce and herbs in pots and window boxes.

At present, I grow enough fresh vegetables for a family of five, and can and preserve half of our annual supply of pickles, relishes, catsup, tomato sauce, tomatoes and tomato juice, peas, green beans, lima beans, peppers, squash and onions — all this on what amounts to 400 square feet of land. My garden consists of narrow three-foot and four-foot strips of soil reclaimed from scraggly lawn along the three sides of tall redwood fencing in our back yard.

After rebuilding the iron-hard adobe soil left packed and filled with construction refuse by the builder of our "apartment cluster," I had to improvise two new gardening rules to surmount the limitations of space and sunlight: (1) follow the sun with successive plantings, and (2) grow everything possible up onto the fences — peas, pole beans, cucumbers and even squash. Chicken wire, trellises and cord netting available from nurseries and garden supply stores all work well.

For gardening in a limited space hemmed by fences or trees, follow the annual north-south movement of the sun each month, calculating just which garden spots will receive the necessary six hours of sunlight during any particular season. Tomatoes, beans, onions, squash, peppers and eggplant need as much sun as possible. Lettuce, cucumbers, spinach, Swiss chard and radishes will flourish in light or partial shade.

Backyard Gardening Tips   Compost all the vegetable matter that comes from your lawn, garden and flower beds. Garden trash such as cornstalks and tomato vines should be composted so that the heat of decomposition kills harmful bacteria and plant-pest eggs. Kitchen scraps (except meat) can be buried directly in the garden. Run the power mower back and forth over piles of leaves; these and grass clippings may be applied directly as mulch or be dug into the soil in winter (see page 275).

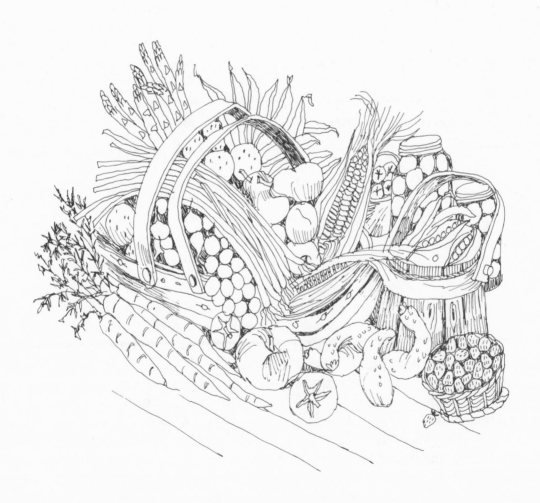

Early – and Fall – Plantings   The cool-weather crops that can be planted one month before the last frost (or as early as February in relatively frost-free areas) are Brussels sprouts, beets, broccoli, cauliflower, cabbage, carrots, kohlrabi, leeks, lettuces, onions, parsnips, potatoes, peas, radishes, rutabaga, spinach, Swiss chard and turnips. These crops, plus green and wax bush beans, can be planted again in midsummer (between August 1st and 15th) for fall maturity.

Warm-Weather Crops   Crops that should be set out after the last frost and when the ground is thoroughly warm are beans, cucumbers, corn, eggplant, melons, okra, pumpkins, peppers, squash and tomatoes. With the exception of corn and beans, these all transplant readily and may be started in hot frames or window sills for quicker maturity.

Interplanting   Interplant fast-growing vegetables with slow-growing ones. Set onion starts around baby cabbage or cauliflower; you can use the onions for scallions before the cabbage matures. Sow an early crop of radishes or Early Alaska peas in the space set aside for beans and tomatoes. Sow beets in spots saved for warm-weather crops and use the beet tops in greens mixtures, both cooked and in salads.

Second Cropping   With composting and
fertilization, garden space need never stand empty. When a
cool-weather crop like lettuce, peas or radishes is done,
replant the area with warm-weather crops such as beans,
squash, peppers or eggplant. Early-maturing corn such as
Early Sunglow (53 days) can follow cool-weather plants.
Stagger plantings of beets, lettuce, radishes and spinach in
one-to-two week intervals to ensure a relatively constant
supply.

Transplanting Tips   Disturb the roots as little as
possible when transplanting. In general, the plant may be
set in the ground just slightly lower than it grew in the pot or
flat. Peat pots, available in all sizes, are excellent for
transplanting, since the whole unit may be set in the
ground. Peat pots not only prevent disturbance to the roots
but also provide nutrients to the plant. The skilled gardener
with sensitive fingers, however, can largely dispense with
peat pots, using them only for eggplant and early tomatoes
that are grown quite large in the windowsill to facilitate
early production. In all cases, keep vegetable seedlings and
transplants moist. Later, as the roots become more
developed, once-weekly watering is sufficient. Ensure,
however, that at least two inches of water penetrate the soil.
Soaker hoses are the best garden waterers.

Insects and Diseases   In over thirty years of gardening, I have never lost a garden, or one crop in a garden, to insects. And, while not a zealous organic gardener, I have always avoided the chemical overkill available in commercial insecticides (and fertilizers!). Fortunately, the most voracious and hard-to-kill garden predators, swarms of grasshoppers, are not much of a problem in California and the Pacific Northwest. Snails, slugs, whitefly, Mexican bean beetles, Colorado potato beetles, squash borers and tomato hornworms are our biggest problems.

Commercial snail and slug bait is the only strong nonorganic insecticide I use. Sturdy, healthy garden plants are the best protection against predatory insects. Tomato hornworms, which can eat a shocking amount of tomato leaves (and half a large green tomato) overnight, are easily discovered and picked off — and the tomato plant suffers no shock whatsoever. Whitefly can be demolished by strong sprays of water directed at the undersides of infested leaves. Squash vines can be rerooted by burying sections of vine with earth every four or five feet, thus thwarting the depredations of the squash borer. Potato beetle larvae can be picked off the plants by hand and disposed of in a can of kerosene. For other persistent plant enemies such as Mexican bean beetles, a spray or powder dusting weekly of 5% Sevin (which breaks down into harmless components readily) or Rotenone or Pyrethrum (which are derived from plants) will provide adequate control.

The alert and curious gardener will notice that certain plants such as marigolds, all herbs and chrysanthemums (a member of the pyrethrum family) not only do not suffer insect damage but actually *repel* insects. I lavishly interplant herbs and French marigolds among vegetables. This not only controls predatory insect populations but also provides an eyecatching diversity of colors and textures in garden beds.

One last note about pest control: Insect damage to your garden plants may be more aesthetic than real. (Some people are just plain outraged: "How dare those little freaks lounge uncontrolled among my broccoli and snap beans!") If the damage is not reducing the edible yield, or if it is slight, you may find living with a few pests preferable to undertaking control measures, especially if they involve using chemicals or other potentially harmful substances.

Onions and Potatoes   I am pretty much a sceptic when it comes to the supernatural, but there are some nonrational tips to gardening that seem to work. Root crops, for example, *do* seem to yield better when planted by the dark of the moon. Equally important, however, are full sun and a loose, preferably sandy, soil. Onions for storage should be allowed to grow near or at the surface. When they mature, knock the tops over and leave for about a week, then dig the onions and allow them to cure in the shade for two to three days. Dig a trench for potatoes and plant the potatoes two inches deep. (For seed, cut potatoes in chunks with one or two eyes to each chunk and let them "cure" for a few days.) As the potato sprouts emerge, pull the hilled-up soil on the sides of the trench down around them. Then, cultivating deeply between the two-foot or three-foot-wide potato rows, pull the soil up with a rake until each potato row is hilled. As the potatoes start to bloom, you may gently probe with your fingers into the hills and pick small new potatoes without harming the plant.

Tomato Tips   The hardiness and sometimes phenomenal productivity of tomatoes give more courage to amateur gardeners than some how-to gardening manuals. And, as supermarkets continue to offer baseball-hard, mealy tomatoes bred more to survive mass transport than for good eating, more and more folks are learning to grow their own.

The Burpee Pixie hybrid is a superb patio, pot or garden tomato which can be grown successfully indoors in winter. It is a sturdy, determinate variety that will robustly spread and produce tennis-ball-size tomatoes in the garden and golf-ball-size tomatoes in a pot indoors.

For extra early tomatoes (before July 1st), start some Pixies indoors in March. Transplanted to the garden around mid-April, they will, given enough sun, produce ripe tomatoes as early as June 1st, well ahead of the regular crop of Rutgers, Beefsteak, Ace and Big Boy.

In the milder climates of California and the Pacific Northwest, garden-ripe tomatoes may be enjoyed up until Christmas. The trick here is to start new plants around the first of August that will bear until the usual November frosts. It is not generally known that you can grow healthy tomato plants from slips. Select one of your mature, healthy plants. Cut away a sucker — the growth that looks like a new miniature plant coming out of the junction of a branch with the main stem. Put the sucker in a glass of water and place it in a sunny indoor location. Within a week it will send out roots, and within two weeks you will have a vigorous root system that may be gently planted in soil in a peat pot and later returned to the garden. This plant will then produce heavily in the late fall when the mature plants have begun to show signs of debility and exhaustion.

Just before the first frost, pull all tomato plants, shake the dirt from the roots, and hang them upside down in a cool spot. Or, pick all the well-developed green tomatoes, wrap them individually in newspaper and store them in boxes in single layers. In both cases, the green tomatoes will ripen naturally over the following month.

Tomatoes respond well to fertilizer, but if over-fertilized with nitrogen-rich material, they will produce more lush vines than blooms. Fertilize well when setting out the plants (and add a little bone meal mixed into the soil beneath the transplant), then forget it until late in the growing season. After the first big crop of tomatoes, fertilize lightly around the plant for the second run.

Staked plants take less space and grow larger and cleaner tomatoes than sprawling ones, but the latter will bear more heavily and over a longer period of time. I stake some varieties for table slicing use and let others grow unchecked for the big preserving crop. Straw or dry-grass mulch will prevent insect damage and rot to tomatoes lying on the damp ground.

The Lettuce Rotation   Lettuce can be grown the
year-round in the coastal climates of California and the
Pacific Northwest. We buy lettuce in the store only three or
four times a year (usually when someone has forgotten the
rhythm of starting seedlings in a window flat each month).

In our coastal climate, lettuce is, oddly enough,
harder to keep growing during the heat of midsummer than
it is during the mild winter months. However, the Burpee
Seed Company has recently developed a superb dark-green
leaf lettuce (Royal Oak) that flourishes right through the
tough, lettuce-wilting heat of summer. The crisp and tender
Royal Oak is also winter-hardy. Lettuce slows considerably
in growth during short winter days, but varieties like Royal
Oak, Romaine and Oak Leaf do quite nicely during cool,
rainy weather and will survive light frosts undamaged.

To avoid the vicissitudes of seasonal fluctuations in
temperature, seed the lettuce in pots or flats in the house.
When it is well up through the soil and has reached about
two inches in height, put the lettuce seedlings outdoors
(only for half a day for the first three days) to "harden off"
the house-born plants. Then transplant them into the
garden, leaving two or three healthy plants in the pot. These
will mature before the transplanted sets.

And raise a number of varieties (avoiding the
tasteless, correct nullity of Iceberg). The tastiest salad
mixtures consist of Salad Bowl, Boston, Bibb, Black-Seeded
Simpson, Royal Oak, Oak Leaf and Romaine — a hungering
variety of colors, textures and tastes. With this plan, you
rarely need to store lettuce in the refrigerator, unless you

overcrop. There's something deeply satisfying about nipping out the door to pluck a few lettuce leaves off a plant to lay into a waiting pastrami sandwich.

There is a wealth of books, magazines and pamphlets available giving full gardening instructions (see page 283); like skiing, however, gardening is best learned from a good instructor. Get to know a successful gardener in your neighborhood. Gardeners love to have their efforts recognized almost as much as they love to talk about gardening.

Most of all, be not discouraged by wet, chilly spells that rot the seed in the ground; varmints (especially gophers, squirrels and rabbits); birds (especially blue jays and starlings, who love to dine both on planted seed and the new shoots); boisterous children; digging dogs and cats; flying and creeping bugs; mold, wilt and rot diseases; drought, wind, flood and hail.

Because the unreasoning earth will always answer with spring.

Back-Yard Escargot

Possibly the earthiest and boldest form of organic gardening is to eliminate your garden pests naturally by eating them. This is less a joke than it appears to be in the case of *Helix aspersa,* the common garden snail.

Helix aspersa is a gastropod, thus belonging to a large family of edible molluscs. Although many folks hardly consider as gastronomic something that crawls across their lawns, our friend *Helix* is that superb, bracingly garlicky, expensive escargot entree served in fine restaurants. Indeed, our garden snails were introduced into California by the French sometime in the mid-1800s. After importing escargot for a century, California is just beginning to be viewed as a possible source of export to snail-hungry Europe. A young Frenchman, Francois Picart, has recently begun collecting, raising and processing escargot for sale in a small operation in Sonoma County.

During one of my semi-annual perusals of that basic treasure of food lore, the *Larousse Gastronomique,* I discovered that *Helix aspersa* were the guys nipping off new lettuce, peas and beans in my garden. Reading further, I discovered how the French fed the snails for plumpness and cleanliness and prepared them for the table. Since that time, our more adventurous house guests have dined elegantly on back-yard escargots at our table.

Preparing Escargot

A month before you intend to eat them, gather large garden snails and put them into a wooden box containing about an inch of cornmeal on the bottom. Cover the box with a piece of screen. In one corner, place a shallow dish with water and a few small rocks in it. Feed the snails every 2-3 days on scraps of lettuce, cabbage and other greens. After a month of this cornmeal– greens diet they are ready to eat.

Boil the snails in their shells for 3-5 minutes. Remove from the water and pull the bodies from the shells. Place snails in a pot and cover with water, adding 1 bay leaf and ½ teaspoon thyme. Boil 30 minutes.

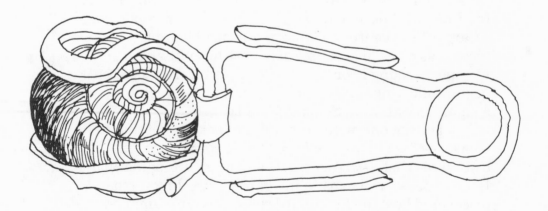

Snail Garlic Sauce

1 cup softened butter (preferably unsalted)
2 to 12 cloves garlic, crushed (depending on taste)
3 tablespoons chopped parsley
1 tablespoon finely chopped chives
1 tablespoon finely chopped shallots
1 teaspoon salt
½ teaspoon pepper
48 cooked escargots

Mix butter and other ingredients together well. Using a ceramic pie plate or shallow casserole dish, pour in some of the sauce, add cooked escargots and top with remaining sauce. Place in a pre-heated 400° oven for about 8 minutes or until hot and bubbly.

Francois Picart is doing a booming business in escargot in Santa Rosa and has prepared for distribution a small booklet on raising, processing and preparing snails. It is available in many West Coast stores where his snails are sold (frozen) or may be ordered from his plant at 1550 Ridley Ave., Santa Rosa, CA.

Making

Spring Salads

Too many American restaurants suffer tunnel vision when it comes to salads. American Indians, and our settler ancestors, living off the land, frequently prepared unusually imaginative salads by gathering what was seasonally available. All of the greens mentioned earlier (pages 11-14), plus violet leaves, marigold petals, chrysanthemum leaves, raw zucchini and Jerusalem artichokes, can provide a lilt of texture and taste to salads.

Dandelion Potato Salad

4 cups cubed, cooked (preferably new) potatoes
4 diced hard-boiled eggs
¼ cup chopped green onions or chives
1 cup dandelion petals and greens

Pick only the small, crisp new dandelion leaves; when plucking the petals, hold the flower firmly to pull the petals to avoid the bitter milk. Toss the ingredients with a mixture of ¼ teaspoon each of celery seed, salt, pepper mixed into ½ cup of mayonnaise. For variety, four slices of diced, crisp-fried bacon can be crumbled into the mixture.

Spoon Salad

Southern Californians long ago found uses for the orange tree in salads. The following letter, tracking down early California salad lore, is from Smokestack El Ropo, formerly associate editor of *Rolling Stone* magazine. Born in Benicia, the first California state capital, and raised in the Los Angeles area, Smokestack possesses an almost encyclopedic knowledge of international food lore.

"Salad. We had a salad with oranges [during his Los Angeles childhood], or rather at least two salads, with oranges that date from before the lime Jell-O period of sweet salads. They were called Summer Salad or Spoon Salad and were meant for hot weather. Don't remember any special name to distinguish the two I remember. ('What's the name of this?' 'Spoon Salad,' said an aunt. 'Yes, that one's Spoon Salad too,' said another aunt. 'What do *we* call it?' 'The one with the walnuts or the one with the cucumbers?' . . .).

"For both, the oranges could be prepared two ways: separating the carpels and peeling off the thin skin from the sides of them and slicing up the carpels as if they were carrots and then mixing the orange pieces with the other ingredients, the whole being served in glass bowls; or simply taking the rind off the orange, leaving the carpels attached and cutting the oranges into the usual orange slices and serving the rest of the salad *on top* of the slices. Much debate over which was the more elegant, with the on-top arrangement prevailing, both because of its suggestion of French restaurant service and because it meant not having to peel the carpels.

"One salad added diced celery and chopped walnuts; the other added instead diced cucumbers and chopped mint. The dressing was the same in both cases: sour cream thinned with the orange juice from the cutting of the oranges (for the clever cook) and at least some water to make a sauce with a salad-dressing consistency. This is in theory; in practice I remember it was often thinned mayonnaise, but always with some added lemon juice so that the dressing would be tart. The sauce is supposed to be light; this is a hot-weather dish.

"We also used to throw orange and lemon leaves into green salad — the leaflets that came out in April and May.

"My grandmother did some foraging for salads. She would go picking greens in Fern Dell at Griffith Park, telling me forcefully that there was nothing wrong in her doing so. Young fiddlehead fern sprouts, miner's lettuce and such. But if anybody stared at her for very long, despite the fact that there wasn't a *thing in the world wrong* with picking some leaves in a public fern dell, she would get huffy and self-righteously whisk us all out of the park as if her virtue had been threatened by a man of low degree. Grandma formed forever my idea of southern womanhood."

Wilted Lettuce

Along with creamed garden peas and new potatoes, wilted lettuce is the true harbinger of spring, when the first tender garden "sass" appears on the table. The Northwestern Indians wilted their spring greens with bear grease and fish oil.

 3 slices bacon
¼ cup vinegar
½ teaspoon salt
 1 teaspoon sugar

Cut bacon into small pieces. Cook slowly until crisp. Stir in vinegar and seasoning. Reheat and pour over lettuce, spinach or any greens. Thinned lettuce from your garden is perfect for this salad; any greens may be mixed with the lettuce. For a lilting variation, add croutons made from your stale bread (toasted in the oven) and 1 tablespoon sesame seeds browned slowly in a little vegetable oil.

Mexican-American Cookery: The Soul Food of California

My earliest memories of community come from the Depression-era San Fernando Valley, just north of Los Angeles. My schoolmates, fellow tomato-pickers and playmates were Mexican-Americans. In the smog-free, sun-drenched valley, covered then not with tract homes but with large truck farms and movie star "ranchos," the very place names were redolent of the Spanish land-grant and Mexican cultural origins of the Los Angeles Plain — towns like Reseda, Canoga Park, Encino and Pacoima; streets and boulevards like Ventura, Sepulveda, Topanga and Pico Rivera; mostly-dry rivers and creeks like Pisco Wash and Arroyo de los Frijoles.

During the year my mother spent convalescing from the difficult delivery of a younger brother, we had a live-in cook and housekeeper. Dolores Sanchez was a fifth-generation Angeleno and was fiercely proud of her lineage; she could trace her family roots back to the first Mexican land-grant families who founded the City of the Angels. Her family still lived just off Olvera Street, the original tile-roofed adobe community that eventually became Los Angeles.

Dolores Sanchez taught my mother how an imaginative variation of crucial spices and peppers multiplied the flavor possibilities of staple Mexican foods — corn, beans and tomatoes. And it was Dolores who inadvertently initiated me into the fiery subtleties of Mexican-American cookery.

One hot, sun-baked San Fernando Valley August day, I was fooling around in the stuffy kitchen, a pottering six-year-old. Dolores, sweating amidst steaming kettles, was canning and stringing for drying a half-bushel of tiny, bright green chile pequines. Chile pequines are probably hot enough to tan horsehide, far more fiery even than Tabasco or jalapeño peppers.

Despite Dolores's repeated admonitions, I insisted on playing with the peppers, lining them up in interesting patterns on the kitchen table.

"You get peppers on your fingers and touch your eyes," Dolores warned, "and they'll burn all day!"

Which the feckless six-year-old ignored, until answering a call to nature a half-hour later. It burned not only all day, precipitating a jittery quickstep, but all night as well, all of which elicited only a cold-hearted "I told you so" from Dolores.

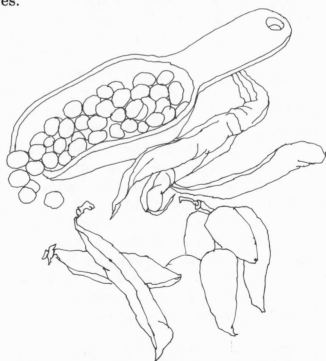

The Heart of the Matter

Because so many Americans have trouble with the frequently fiery nature of Mexican spices and peppers, Mexican food is more corrupted into blandness than any other ethnic food in America. Equipped, however, with a sure knowledge of the range and varieties of Mexican peppers and spices, one can ensure piquancy in flavor without necessarily burning the tongue.

American chili, for instance, from anywhere north of San Antonio to Seattle to Bangor, is usually a bland boil of cumin, tomato sauce, garlic and hamburger. Good chili, with its complex of flavors, requires both red and green chiles and boiled, shredded beef or coarsely ground chuck rather than hamburger. The meats of Mexico tend to be tough but flavorful — goat, mutton, grass-and-cactus-fed beef and barn-yard chicken. As a result, most Mexican and Mexican-American dishes call for a precooked, tenderized cut of meat or for long simmering in a flavorful sauce, as in the case of *posole* and *menudo* (page 60).

Cumin is the distinctive "Mexican" flavor most Americans recognize as characteristic of Mexican food. But over forty varieties of chiles are commonly used as subtle spices in the cookery of Mexico.

Most of these peppers may be grown in the warmer regions of California. (They may also be purchased in Mexican-American communities from San Diego north to the Central Valley.) Peppers are among the easiest-grown of garden vegetables — they flourish in poor soil and require little care. However, they are easily over-watered and over-fertilized, which leads to more leaf growth than peppers. The only other problem with peppers is that they definitely require warm weather. If set out in the garden too soon, or if they experience a cold spell early in the growing season, they often go into a sulk, doing nothing for as long as a month. Be patient.

All peppers (except bell peppers) are easily dried, and all may be frozen directly without blanching. To dry, string ripe, red peppers on a stout thread, piercing each pepper with a needle at the base of the stem to ensure that they do not hang in contact with one another and mold. Hang outdoors in the sun or in a sunny window for a few months.

Anaheim   The long, green, mildly-hot pepper used for rellenos and the "diced green chiles" canned commercially. Should be added to tamale pie, posole, chili and Mexican hominy. They turn bright red when ripe and dry well, imparting a fresh pepper taste without being overly hot. The skins should be removed from green Anaheims when used in rellenos or when canned, but it is an exasperating process. To skin, spread the peppers on a cookie sheet and put under the broiler until they scorch (turn black) and the skin raises off the flesh. Turn the peppers over and repeat. The skins may then be peeled off or rubbed off with a towel. Frozen Anaheims skin quite easily when thawed, but the freezing tenderizes them so much they do not hold together well for dishes such as rellenos.

Fresno   A small, green pepper that turns quite hot when ripe and red. Excellent for drying and crumbling into recipes when hot pepper spice is needed. Not as hot as the better-known jalapeños, Fresno peppers are superb for dicing while green and adding to casseroles and scrambled eggs, or for scattering over fried eggs or adding to a roast beef sandwich. A bright fresh *green* taste. Fresnos make excellent hot peppers when pickled. Simply pierce peppers several times with a pin, pack into a pint jar and cover with hot vinegar. The vinegar pepper sauce is zesty when sprinkled on green beans, ham and navy beans, black-eyed peas or roast pork. Pepper sauce is quite popular in the American South, where the use originated with American Indians of the Southeast and Southwest.

Chipotle and *Adobo*   Canned, processed peppers widely used in Mexico. Chipotles are smoked; adobos are prepared in a red sauce. Both are scorchingly hot.

Cilantro (Chinese parsley, or coriander)   This easily grown herb is a basic Mexican and Mexican-American spice and an essential ingredient in most Mexican-American sauces. Fresh cilantro has a rank odor that, however, does not show up as such after cooking.

Chili powders   Most commercially prepared chili powders are combinations of ground red chiles, cumin and garlic powder. Among the best for power and balance are Grandma's and Gebhardts. They function well as the seasoning base in many Mexican-American dishes, but need to be supplemented with varying amounts of cumin, cilantro and garlic. The best chili powders are the pure ground chiles in clear plastic bags labeled "California Chili," "New Mexico Chili" or "Pasilla Chili." New Mexico chili is the hottest and spiciest; Pasilla is flavorful, rich and mild. Many cooks add one tablespoon of Pasilla chili to any other chili powder used.

Masa

Masa is the basic ground or pounded hominy paste, the staff of life, used in tortillas, tamales and tamale pie. Since masa is prepared from fresh, soft hominy, it does not keep well, molding easily, and is not often stocked by grocery stores. Quaker Masa Harina, a hominy flour, is readily available, but it is only adequate, and not at all equal in flavor and texture to fresh masa. Fresh masa is available for home cookery in many Mexican-American communities in San Diego, Los Angeles, San Jose, San Francisco and in the Central Valley — usually in neighborhood Mexican grocery stores or in Mexican delicatessens.

When living in the Midwest I was able to locate masa in Mexican communities in railroad towns in Kansas and Missouri. For instance, the finest Mexican-American restaurant in Kansas City, Missouri, Los Corrales, makes its own hominy and fresh masa in the restaurant basement, leaching 100 pounds of yellow corn at a time in lye water to remove the outer hull, then grinding the soft, pale-yellow centers into coarse paste.

Angeleno Tamale Pie

Dolores Sanchez claimed that her tamale pie recipe came to Los Angeles with the earliest Mexican families who settled there in the 1830s. Certainly it has a deep flavor and masa crustiness not found in the Americanized casserole cookbook versions of tamale pie. This recipe is obviously for a large family dinner; the amounts may be cut proportionately.

Masa Crust

5 pounds fresh masa (or make from Masa Harina, following instructions on the sack — basically, 2 cups Harina to 1 cup water)
1 tablespoon salt
1 cup Crisco
¼ cup chile puree

In a large bowl, mix all by hand. Line a large greased pan (a roaster is best) with ½ inch of the masa mix. Reserve enough masa mix to cover the mixture with a ½-inch crust.

Filling

5 pounds lean beef
1 soup bone
1 #303 can green chiles or diced green chiles (minus ½ cup
    for crust)
4 large cloves garlic, minced
4 tablespoons cumin seed
2 teaspoons cilantro
1 can ripe, pitted olives
½ cup raisins

Barely cover meat with water in a large skillet; cover
and simmer until tender (about 2 hours). During last half
hour, puree chiles in blender. Add chiles, garlic, cumin seed,
cilantro, olives and raisins. Salt to taste. When meat is
tender, pull apart into bite-sized chunks with a fork.
Thicken the mixture slightly by stirring in a small amount
of corn meal previously mixed with cold water. Remove the
soup bone and pour the meat mixture into the masa-lined
pan. Cover with top crust of masa mix. With a knife, slice a
few holes in the crust for expansion. Bake in 350° oven for 1
hour or until brown and bubbly.

Tamales

The canned and frozen tamales in the supermarket
are a complete travesty of what a tamale should be: grease
instead of spicy sauce; mushy cornmeal instead of firm
masa. The good tamale must be handmade — a complex
process that, however, can become an enjoyable communal
effort. In our case, two families get together for a half-day to
make and enjoy the fresh tamales and divide the remainder
for freezing (tamales freeze well). These are remarkably
inexpensive. We make them with cheaper or bargain meats
— pork shoulder, chicken or turkey legs and beef chuck — or
mashed pinto beans (or mashed pinto beans mixed with any
meat used). Children enjoy the corn-shuck rolling and get
quite good at it. The process as described sounds complicated
but is not, really. This recipe yields about two dozen
tamales.

Masa Mixture

2 pounds fresh masa	*Or*	4 cups Masa Harina
2 tablespoons chili powder		2 cups stock from the meat mixture
4 tablespoons shortening or lard		4 tablespoons shortening or lard
4 teaspoons salt		2 tablespoons chili powder
		4 teaspoons salt

Mix thoroughly by hand or electric mixer.

Meat Mixture

2 pounds lean, boneless pork (or turkey, chicken, beef chuck
    or ground beef) or 4-pound pork shoulder
4 tablespoons chili powder
2 teaspoons cumin powder
2 teaspoons cilantro
1 teaspoon cayenne pepper
2 teaspoons black pepper
2 teaspoons salt
4 cloves garlic, minced
1 bay leaf
1 teaspoon oregano

Cut meat into fairly large chunks and cover with 2 quarts water in a kettle. Simmer for 45 minutes or until tender. Remove bones and skim off excess fat. Reserve the stock.

Put meat through grinder. Add seasonings and 1½ cup stock to the ground meat and mix well.

Soak 50 to 60 dried corn shucks for several hours in hot water. These are available in packages (quite inexpensive) in the Mexican food section of most West Coast supermarkets. Lay out a corn shuck and spread 2 tablespoons of masa mix in a ⅛-inch-thick square from the near edge, leaving an inch of shuck clear at each end and on the far edge. Spoon a heaping tablespoon of meat mixture on top of the masa; then roll tamale like a cigarette, using a second shuck under the far edge if necessary. Fold the shuck ends back along the tamale to seal, or tie with string or strips of corn shuck. Roll rather loosely to allow for swelling of the masa when steamed. Pack tamales standing up in a steamer and steam over boiling water for 1 hour. Reheat for serving by steaming or heating gently in a saucepan.

Note: Scraps of corn shucks cooked with the meat improve the flavor. Mashed pinto beans may be substituted for the meat. In this case, mash the seasonings into the cooked beans. Or the meat may be stretched by putting a scant tablespoon of meat mixture and a scant tablespoon of beans in the tamales.

Chili Verde and Posole

There are two popular Mexican-American versions of a basic Mexican green-chile, soul-food stew — the sturdy, plebeian *menudo,* made with beef tripe, and its more elegant cousin, *posole.* Both are hearty, spicy stews with fresh hominy. Posole has become practically synonymous with New Mexico cookery, but it is prepared in Mexican-American communities throughout the Southwest.

Chili Verde

6 to 8 pork steaks, cubed, or 2½ pounds cubed pork shoulder
3 tablespoons bacon or salt pork fat
3 cloves garlic, minced
1 medium onion, chopped
2 7-ounce cans diced green chiles, or four whole Anaheim
      chiles, diced
1 teaspoon cilantro
2 teaspoons cumin
Salt and pepper to taste

Brown pork in bacon fat; add garlic and onion and fry until soft and transparent. Add remaining ingredients and 1 quart water. Salt and pepper to taste. Simmer for 4 to 6 hours, until meat is *completely* tender. The longer this simmers the richer the taste.

Posole

Just before the chili verde is done, thicken slightly by stirring in a small amount of corn meal mixed with cold water. Prepare the hominy by gently frying a #303 can of hominy and ½ cup chopped green onions, tops and all, in 2 tablespoons bacon or salt pork fat, stirring occasionally. Salt and pepper to taste, then stir hominy into chili verde. Serve the posole in soup bowls.

Huevos Rancheros

Huevos Rancheros is the Mexican and Mexican-American all-purpose breakfast, dinner, lunch and brunch dish. Huevos admits to as many variations as pizza, but there are two inflexible requirements in preparation: The tortillas must be perfectly fried just to the edge of crispness to soak up the egg yolk effectively; and the eggs must be basted sunny side up to have the right loose-yolk consistency to blend with the tortillas. This is an excellent, rib-sticking, high-energy Sunday brunch, especially when accompanied by a stout, dark Mexican beer like Dos Equis or Bohemia.

2 tortillas per person
2 tablespoons vegetable oil
1 7-ounce can green chile salsa (for 2 persons)
Eggs

Heat vegetable oil (or shortening) in a skillet. Quickly fry the tortillas about 1 minute per side, or until lightly crisp around the edges. Drain tortillas on paper towels or newspaper and place on heated plates. Heat the green chile salsa in a saucepan. Fry the eggs sunny side up, basting continuously. Put eggs (1 per tortilla) on tortillas and pour heated salsa over all. Country sausage or link sausage goes well with this. For variations, sprinkle shredded Jack cheese over the eggs, or add 4 tablespoons enchilada sauce to the green chile salsa, or sauté green onions to top the eggs, or do all three. Put a bottle of Tabasco sauce or Salsa Picante on the table.

Cindy-Irene's Primal Chicken Chili Verite

Contrary to the passionate arguments of chili devotees, there is no *best* chili, as there is no best symphony, or novel, or painting. Ultimate delight depends on the personal preferences of the eater. In my opinion, however, real chili should remain true to the basic chile-pepper-and-spice varieties of Mexican cookery.

Such is my wife's Primal Chicken Chili Verite. Cindy-Irene is a Yankee-bred lass who grew up near Milwaukee. Like many Californians, our food predilections are shaped by Midwestern memories. I also cook fairly regularly, and between us we turn out a cuisine that could be called Yankee-Rebel-Tex-Mex. Cindy-Irene is whimsical, subtle, patient and inventive with sauces Hollandaise, Béarnaise, Mousseline. I am the grits, biscuits and gravy man.

The regional differences create an amiable tension in our relationship. Cindy will tolerate grits only in small amounts — sprinkled liberally with garlic salt. And I once referred to her chili, made with kidney beans and, among other things, celery, as "Yankee chili."

"Yankee chili! He called it Yankee chili!" she once mourned loudly to a visiting friend, sounding as if she had discovered tarnish on her wedding ring. "The chili I grew up with and loved as a child, and he tells me it isn't true chili at all!"

Some time later, Cindy-Irene began poring over French and Mexican cookbooks. She carefully sampled sauces in a number of Napa and San Francisco Mexican restaurants. I sensed a plot forming and I wasn't wrong.

"I'm entering the *Rolling Stone* Chili Cook-Off," she announced one day. "It'll be a chicken chili for the Free-Style category. After all, there's chicken tamales, enchiladas and *mole*, so there should be chicken chili." Her logic was as firm as her determination.

Bringing her symbiotic relationship with sauces to bear, Cindy-Irene spent most of the following Saturday at the stove and, a day later, prepared and nervously entered a triumphant chicken chili — handily winning First Prize in the Free-Style category of the *Rolling Stone* Chili Cook-Off of 1976.

Later, polishing her silver trophy and placing it on the mantel, she looked at me and observed acidly, "*Yankee* chili, indeed!"

Chicken Chili Verite

1 whole stewing chicken or fryer
1 #2 can peeled tomatoes, chopped fine
1 10-ounce can enchilada sauce (mild or hot)
1 clove garlic, minced
1 large onion, chopped
½ bell pepper, chopped
4 tablespoons chili powder
1 teaspoon crushed red pepper
1 teaspoon cilantro
1 tablespoon salt
½ teaspoon oregano
½ teaspoon ginger
3 tablespoons cornmeal

Simmer the chicken until tender. Discard skin; remove meat from bones and dice. Reserve chicken stock. Sauté onion, garlic and bell pepper in oil until soft. Add remaining ingredients and simmer gently for 1 hour. Add chicken stock if necessary to maintain chili sauce consistency. Mix cornmeal in small amount of water and stir into chili to thicken during last 15 minutes.

Serve over rice or with pinto beans. If cooked with beans, add 2 cups cooked beans after the first half hour of simmering. Cook pinto beans in the chicken stock and water. Do not salt beans until finished cooking, as salt makes bean skins tough.

Trash Fishing

Spring gardening and fishing have been tangled up in my head ever since those boyhood farm days when, after we broke open deep furrows behind the mule-drawn hand plow for late-March potato planting, my father excused me from further gardening chores to run to the Sac River in the Missouri Ozarks. During the spring spawning run up the river to the grist-mill dam at Caplinger Mills, I caught, netted and sold hundreds of pounds of carp, buffalo, drum, red-horse sucker and blue and channel catfish. One of the old-timers on the porch of the General Store in Caplinger Mills finally allowed as how I was one of the best "trash fishermen" in the river valley.

I was proud of that. Since then, I have stolen away from spring gardening to trash fish, man and boy, from East Texas swamps and Arkansas cypress bayous to Ozark streams and the San Francisco waterfront.

Where others went for northern pike, smallmouth bass and trout, I went for buffalo, carp, paddlefish (spoonbill catfish) and red-horse suckers. Where fishing savants offered handtied flies, silver spoons and rigged anchovies, I tossed sticky catalpa worms, chicken guts and stink bait.

Stink bait. Like much else in our convenience-food society, they don't make it like they used to. The commercial preparations available in bait shops nowadays contain any number of harmful additives trying to emulate the bewitching effluence of rotting meat. My Ozark recipe for stink bait, which I got from Bill Keith in 1946, is the only certain nemesis of catfish, carp and human olfactory nerves known to man.

Bill Keith and his brother Mattie were two bachelors who lived in a two-room dogtrot cabin in a narrow limestone and cedar hollow near our farm outside Caplinger Mills, Missouri. Bill and Mattie raised hounds, made whiskey, hunted coons, trapped muskrats and netted trash fish from the Sac River, in that order. Bill was the quiet, passive and friendly dog raiser. Mattie was pure mean slit-eyed redneck. He made the whiskey back in the woods and packed a .22 automatic pistol. Mattie was known to shoot at strangers in his woods.

Underneath the Keith brothers' cabin, which was built on a foundation of eight stone pillars, lived a moiling mob of milk goats, banty chickens and a magnificent clutch of Walker, Redbone, Black-and-Tan and Blue-Tick hounds, plus a fyce or two.

It was simple hill-country gratitude that prompted Bill Keith to give up his treasured stink-bait recipe. It was the winter he took to his bed with a month-long bout of the ague. My mother, despairing of Bill Keith ever seeing a doctor, sent me over to his cabin with a lard bucket full of hot squirrel stew and a bottle of cough medicine. Bill had his rumpled double bed pulled up next to the open fireplace. Two Black-and-Tans and a Redbone hound were butted up against him, snoozing on the bed.

"Them damn hounds bring in fleas, but they purely do keep me warm," he explained, pouring the cough medicine into a tumbler glass half-full of clear homemade whiskey that was already next to his bed.

Bill blinked his watery red eyes, coughed off the jolt of raw whiskey, scratched at the baggy crotch of his iron-gray long johns and eyed me in a measuring sort of way.

"Tell your Ma I'm gonna give y'all me'n Mattie's stink-bait recipe. You tell anybody else, Mattie'll skin you like a slough mushrat. This here bait keeps us in the trash-fish bidness.

"Now you take a Vieeny-sausage can of yellow cornmeal, add a half-can of cut-up cracker cheese, two fresh cottontail rabbit livers, a big spit of Day's Work or Beech-Nut chewin' tobacco, plus the chewed-up plug, an' a little cotton to stick it all together. Then bury it in the ground in a glass jar, best durin' the full of the moon, for two weeks of age on it."

That was the recipe. A lump of this bait the size of a black walnut is then pressed onto a treble hook and tossed out to any cruising blue catfish or pale buffalo in the slow backwaters of a thick American river. (Real trash fishermen avoid currents and clear, running water. Hang out at a riffle in a sparkling mountain stream, they'd say, and you'll likely fall into the company of fast and glib, uptown fly and lure fishermen who really aren't open to the nuances of trash fishing.)

After Bill Keith, my next trash fishing guru was a neighborhood bachelor in Emporia, Kansas, by the name of Litter Louie. Litter Louie was a small, swarthy, saturnine retired Portuguese farm worker who trash fished on the Cottonwood and Neosho rivers outside town. We called him Litter Louie because he always threw the fish heads from his day's catch out on his front door steps for the neighborhood cats. Litter Louie's front steps sported some of the most awesome technicolored cat fighting this side of Bombay, India.

Louie didn't speak much to anyone on the street, but he accosted me one day as I was stowing a seven-foot fly rod in my car.

"Hey, guy, where you goin' with that damn telephone pole?"

"Well, ah, thought I'd try for brown bass out in the Fling Hills," I replied defensively.

Louie squinted at the sun, then thoughtfully hefted the bulging gunny sack he usually carried over the shoulder of his stained denim jacket.

"C'mon, I got enough chicken livers for the both of us. I'll show ya how to catch enough bullhead to fill that there car trunk."

Besides that, Louie showed me every buffalo, carp and catfish hole in the Cottonwood River, from Emporia upstream to Florence. He also showed me how to fillet buffalo, smoke carp and deep-fry catfish.

Louie insisted on fishing gear that was solid, simple and direct: a stiff, stubby bait or spinning rod, 40-pound test line for retrieving bait from underwater stumps and drift piles of timber, solid four-ounce lead sinkers, and treble hooks to hold firmly the soft bait — liver, corn, chicken guts or stink bait.

Louie also taught me to think like a catfish, to drift bait through a riffle on full-moon nights when channel and flathead cats, the sport fish of the trash fish family, would swarm to the pools below the riffles to hit anything moving in the current.

Finally, Litter Louie took me on a now-legendary trip south to Chetopa, Kansas, on the banks of the Neosho River snug against the Kansas–Oklahoma border. "The Catfish Capital of the World!" claims the weathered banner across Chetopa's empty main street — and it is. Betimes napping in rolled-up blankets beside an all-night campfire and nipping regularly from a jug of Heaven Hill bourbon, we drifted big red-horse sucker minnows through a deep, gravelly riffle a few miles north of town. We came home with over 150 pounds of channel catfish, all filleted out and packed on ice for an Emporia fish fry.

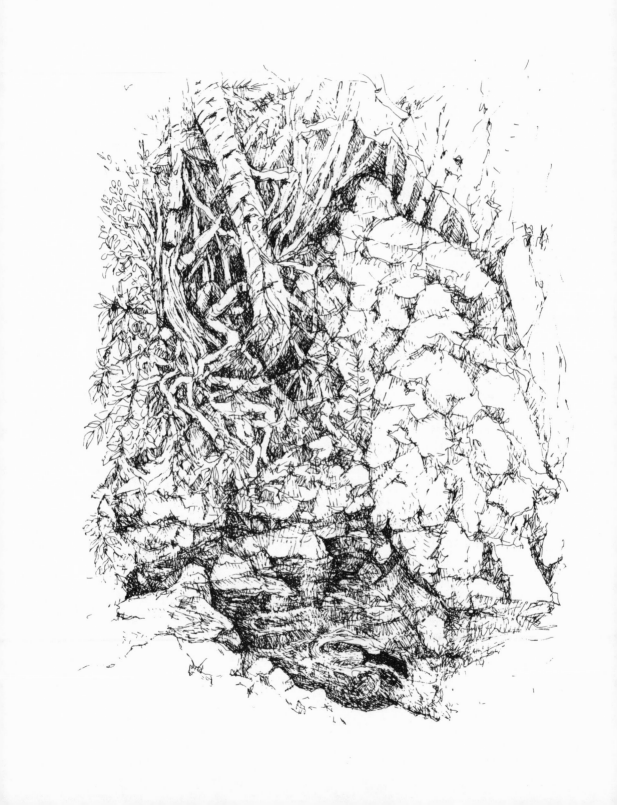

There is an easy camaraderie and lazy tolerance in trash fishing society. But even trash fishing has its pecking order, and at the bottom of that is the most desperate, country-dumb form of fishing to be found since Cro-Magnon times: noodling.

Noodling is wading, swimming or floundering around in the mud, rotted vegetation and flotsam-jetsam of a river or creek, feeling in bank holes and under rocks and logs for big, lethargic catfish.

If you ease up to a resting catfish and gently stroke it on its side, it becomes mesmerized into immobility. The trick of noodling is then to slip your hand alongside the head . . . slowly . . . then hook your thumb into the gill opening, and voila! Catfish fillets! Rolled in buttermilk and cornmeal, deep-fried in lard for supper! Along with hush-puppies, fried potatoes and onions and a mess of poke greens, this is what we trash fishermen know as "American macrobiotic."

Roy Brashears once took me noodling and cured me of noodling all in the same day. Roy Brashears was the champion noodler of Putnam County, in the north-central Missouri hill country. There, the muddy, catfish-rich Chariton River twists and yearly floods its way through Putnam County. Serious trash fishermen on the Chariton around Livonia, Missouri (population 600), set limb lines for sixty-pound blue cats by impaling a skinned rabbit on a hook the size of a grown man's hand and tying it with sash cord to a limber willow sapling on the riverbank.

Roy Brashears was a dashing ol' boy who returned to Livonia early from World War II with a handful of medals and a chestful of angry red scars from winning a serious argument with two German machine gun emplacements outside St. Lô in France. Big in a soft, shambling Slim Pickens sort of way, Roy wasn't afraid of anything. We older high school boys were especially proud of the way he drove our '41 Ford V-8 school bus flat out at 65, slewing grandly down mut-rut lanes and gravel county roads.

"That Roy Brashears," marvelled Loy Hicks, the day he pulled our canted-over bus out of a river-bottom drainage ditch with his two-banger John Deere tractor, "that Roy Brashears is just gonna tear hell off the cross, ain't he?"

Then Roy discovered that I had learned the basics of noodling from my uncles. "Reckon young Tex here is old enough to find his own poke-holes?" is the way Roy put it, winking broadly at the other Saturday idlers watching me get a haircut in Roy's daddy's barber shop in Livonia.

Roy spit a long, brown stream of Day's Work into the ashbox in front of the woodstove and contentedly watched it sizzle away.

"Best poke-holes for noodlin' is in the Shoal Crick hole," offered Harmon Sipes, who farmed over in the Gooseneck Bend area of the Chariton.

"Yep," Roy agreed. He stretched up and tucked his black Can't Bust 'Em jeans into the tops of his orange cowboy boots. "Me'n Tex here is gonna noodle out some of them big fat blue cats sleepin' in that hole."

So there were four of us, barefooted and in gallus overalls, on the Chariton riverbank that next warm, lace-green April morning — each with a ten-foot sash cord fish stringer wrapped around his waist. The minute I stepped off the silt sandbar into the oozy river bottom, a six-inch black locust thorn went half-way through my foot.

"Blue mud!" yelled Roy. "Pack it with blue mud off that bank there. Blue mud'll draw the poison right out!"

In five feet of water, Roy had his belly against the mud bank as he sidled downstream. The bank was full of holes gouged by the heavy March runoff.

"Oof!" Roy whooped. "That sucker musta weighed twenty, I bet. Hit me in the stomach like a damn freight train going to the roundhouse."

I angled a protective elbow over my stomach, trying to ignore my throbbing right foot as I began gingerly to feel back into the underwater holes. Underfoot were squishy soft-shell turtles. There were, we knew, forty-pound snapping turtles half-buried in the river-bottom mud, although no one in Putnam County knew of anyone ever being bitten by a snapper *while in the water.* And there was the occasional ominous plop of a harmless water snake — or water moccasin — slithering off an overhanging sycamore branch.

"Uh-oh," Roy muttered, as we worked downstream, half-laying on the slippery bank. He sucked in his breath. "Here's a big daddy flathead, an' I . . ."

He broke off, half whirled in a jerky way and went under water. The three of us laughed. This here crazy Roy Brashears, a ring-tailed noodler, swimmin' right down there into catfish holes to rassle a big daddy flathead catfish!

But Roy wasn't in the hole, or along the bank. In a boil of water, mud and spray, he shot up into the air mid-river, hollering and choking.

"Th'ow me a rope! Sonofabitch got *me,* got my whole *arm!*" he yelled, in a strangled sort of way. He flailed wildly with his left arm and raced in a herky–jerky manner about the surface of the river.

Before we could even pull our feet out of the river mud he disappeared again. The three of us lunged, swimming towards the bubbles and roiled water where Roy had been.

He surfaced once more, another ten yards downstream, this time swinging a blackened club in his left hand which he had broken off a snag or pulled out of the river bottom, we guessed.

It seemed a strange, inexplicable, violent dream. Roy had gone crazy, or some kind of mud monster was trying to drag him into the deepest murk of the Chariton. Roy bellowed and poked violently into the water with his club. By now his flopping exertions had carried him to the shelving bottom of a silt bar that marked the lower end of the long Shoal Creek hole. Roy staggered around on his feet and, his body jerked to left and right by the strange force underwater, splashed towards the dark beach.

Then we saw it. A huge, thrashing flathead catfish, half as long as Roy himself, hung from his right arm.

Roy's forearm, up to the elbow, disappeared into the catfish's mouth.

We floundered out onto the bar, bug-eyed. We hadn't any idea what to do. Roy stood there with his arm in the fish's mouth. It had quit thrashing. It just hung there. Roy's face was pasty white; he was spitting gouts of water and trembling all over.

"It hurt, Roy?" was all I could think to say.

"Naw, only where he's chomping on it," Roy said, twisting around and clawing at his left hip pocket with his free hand. He pulled out a six-inch folding jacknife, opened it with his teeth, and began prying with the flat blade against the fish's jaws. It opened its mouth and flopped to the sand. The top of Roy's arm, from elbow to wrist, was raw and oozing blood. A catfish has, instead of teeth, a wide plate inside both jaws with the texture of triple-deep, garnet sandpaper. The mouth of a speckled-gray flathead catfish is as wide as its flat head.

Already Roy was swaggering, stringing up his fish and admiring it.

"Git me some of that blue mud on this," Roy claimed, waving his bloody arm, "an' we'll noodle us a whole *mess* of catfish. Only, I'm goin' *alongside* the next big-un I grab. I shoulda knowed better than to stick my thumb in his *mouth*."

He shook his head in self-disgust and eased back into the water.

Even today, folks along the upper Chariton River still date time against "that spring ol' Roy Brashears like to got drownded by a 25-pound flathead cat in the Shoal Crick hole. Then it rained pitchforks an' saw-logs for two weeks an' washed out that hole."

I leave noodling to snapping turtles, cottonmouth water moccasins and other low life. Springtime these days I meet with city trash-fishing friends down in San Francisco, along the Pier 32 waterfront next to the Java House Cafe, with six-packs of beer and cut-up anchovy bait, to finesse out sacks-full of starry flounder, rubber-lips and surf perch. Meanwhile, along the soggy banks of the Blue River in northern Kansas, beside the clear, light coffee-colored Gasconade River in the Missouri Ozarks and from the limestone ledges along the lower Pedernales River in south Texas, the trash fishermen of American unlimber their sturdy equipment.

Reeking of beer, stink bait, catalpa worms and cut anchovies, we paddle against the current, seeking that receding dream, a trash fish as big as the Ritz.

SUMMER

Dry Valley

Few things bloom
in a California dry summer
through the dust and parched wild oats.
Outside my cabin,
purple-belled fuchsia
and a few stalks
of volunteer celery
draw bright hummingbird
thrumming the air
down laurel-green hillside.

Splashing red, Clown Fool circles
from purple fuchsia to fern-damp grotto,
ignoring heat and dust,
the supplicating dry oats and fennel.

Family Reunion

Elmer Davids, my maternal grandfather, was a descendant of the English-Scots border Protestants who emigrated to Virginia in the eighteenth century. In 1880, Elmer Davids moved his wife, infant daughter and household effects by covered wagon from Indiana to his father's log cabin outside Unionville, Missouri.

The family homesteaded 160 acres of steep wooded hills and fertile creek-bottom land five miles west of Livonia. Elmer Davids built a two-story log cabin of foot-square, hand-hewn black walnut logs. He and Edna raised ten children; one daughter died of typhoid fever and a son was kicked to death by a horse.

Elmer Davids was a quiet, gentle, white-bearded man who died more from overwork than anything else. He cropped the land, mined coal from nearby hillsides and raised, slaughtered and preserved all of his family's meat. Helping him tend his ten hives of bees, we learned that he yearly planted five acres of buckwheat mostly for the bees and the fine, tangy honey it produced.

Some of the Davids children followed the last westering migrations of the Depression and World War II, but many of them remained close to the home place.

Summer is family reunion time in those tumbled green hills, where time seems to go slower and family ties are more easily maintained than they are in places where people lead faster-paced lives. The Davids family reunion has been an unbroken event for more than forty-five years, though until last summer I hadn't attended one since the 1950s. As I parked the dusty car with California plates on the quiet dirt street on the edge of Kirksville, my new wife, Cindy-Irene, was somewhat apprehensive about being accepted.

"Land sakes, child," said Aunt Irene when we got to the house, "we ain't nothin' but old hillbillies." She took Cindy-Irene by the hand. "You come right here in the kitchen with me and I'll fix you a glass of iced tea. And have some of those applesauce cookies. Your Aunt Mattie baked them this mornin'."

The men sat out the heat of the humid June afternoon on the front porch shaded by two century-old red oak trees. They worried about the dry spell and the tasseling corn crop. Newly arriving cousins exchanged travel notes and joshed one another about increasing patches of gray hair in the temples.

"Jesse Paul, I knew you was comin', so I baked you a loaf of light-bread," sang Cousin Virgy through the screen door leading into the fragrant house.

Aunt Irene busied herself in the kitchen with homemade noodles, which were drying into pale yellow curls on the kitchen table. They would soon join the steaming, plump chicken in the big pot on the back of the stove.

Cindy-Irene wondered about the bright color of the chicken.

"That's 'cause that chicken was fresh-killed and dressed this mornin'," said Aunt Irene. "Honey, you wouldn't *never* catch me buyin' one a' them pale store chickens!"

Next day, the country food covered a forty-foot row of tables in the Unionville City Park 4-H pavilion. There was the usual friendly competiton between Aunt Irene's and Cousin Margie's chicken and noodles.

"Now everybody dig in," said lanky, red-headed Cousin Oscar after he delivered grace. "Nobody ever went hungry at a Davids family reunion."

After dinner it was storytelling time, while the children played Red Rover and hide-and-seek in the park. The head of each family stood and spoke of the year's events and how the children and grandchildren and great-grandchildren were doing. The three Davids girls present told stories on one another about the distant time when they were high-spirited farm girls. "It was rainin' pitchforks and sawlogs," began Aunt Irene, laughing, telling the story of Aunt Merle falling off Old Fly.

Escaping the heat of the park building, about forty of us went over to Uncle Marion's house. One group, drowsily working off the effects of the huge dinner, pitched horseshoes in the peony-dappled shade of an old wild cherry tree. We swapped fishing and hunting stories and heard again about the biggest catfish ever taken out of the nearby Chariton River.

Another group gathered around the piano in the back parlor. They sang the songs they grew up with: "The Hills of Home," "Shall We Gather at the River?" "Climbing Jacob's Ladder" and "Will the Circle Be Unbroken?"

Most of us cousins are grandparents now. But for a day last summer we could see again, behind one another's eyes, the free and easy, handsome children we once were when we ran the woods, waded Shoal Creek and played together in the hayloft on rainy days.

Struttin' to the Barbecue

The creative diversity of regional American cookery is nowhere more evident than at the barbecue. Indeed, arguments over barbecue methods generally create a lighthearted regional bigotry in our fair land.

In North Carolina they barbecue beef brisket or pork shoulder, chop the cooked meat into small chunks and mix it in a tangy sauce (often a carefully guarded secret). In Louisiana they add a hot sauce to smoked link sausages that brings a start of tears to the eyes. In Texas they favor slow barbecuing of large slabs of beef. In Kansas City and the Missouri Ozarks, slabs of "long-ends" and "short-ends" pork ribs suspended from revolving spits march slowly through the hickory smoke.

All of these methods appeared in California and the Pacific Northwest with the earliest settlers from those regions. But the settlers of Los Angeles, San Jose, Oregon's Willamette Valley and Washington's Yakima Valley found a long-established barbecue culture among native Indians and, in Southern California, among the Spanish and Mexican-Americans. To the coastal Indians of the Pacific Northwest, the finest barbecue meant salmon, split flat and held by green willow or alder withes, slowly grilled over oak, maple or alder coals (see pages 201-204). Larger haunches of deer and bear meat were cooked in the middle of three small fires which ensured that the meat was thoroughly slow-roasted. The Indians of Southern California — and the early Spanish and Mexican settlers — knew the gustatory delights of barbecuing goat, mutton and beef over slow fires of manzanita and mesquite charcoal.

The barbecue method discussed here is native American pit barbecue, a cooking method that stands midway between slow smoking and charcoal grilling — a technique indigenous to California and the Pacific Northwest that was later refined by early settlers from other barbecuing regions.

The pit barbecue method creates a fully cooked, tender, juicy slab of ribs, beef roast or pork shoulder that is permeated to the core with tangy, addictive sweet smoke flavor. Quick charcoal grilling, which tends to produce a black, gummy crust of congealed sauce, only shows how far we have wandered from the American frontier faith of hand-rubbed, corncob-and-apple-smoked ham, home-ground sausage and smoked wild turkey.

By virtue of its historical tradition and its ability to redeem tough or cheap cuts of meat, barbecue qualifies as a native American soul food. Aside from lamb, which is barbecued superbly the world over, beef brisket and pork ribs are the finest barbecue meats, chiefly because of the juiciness created by interleaved layers of fat. Other than a ham or occasional chicken or turkey, we rarely consign the better cuts of meat, especially of beef, to the barbecue. Marinated chuck steak, cooked slowly, will barbecue just as tender and juicy as far more expensive porterhouse and T-bone steaks.

The Sauce

No barbecue sauce made by a nationwide distributor is acceptable. The tomato, bless its rosy, red hide, does not belong in barbecue sauce — at least never more than a soupçon per gallon. The inescapable flavor of tomatoes can often blot out subtle meat flavors. Also, the sauce should never be added to the meat until the last fifteen to twenty minutes of the cooking process. It should, of course, be applied liberally to the meat when it is served.

Pit Barbecue Sauce

Ask the butcher for marrow bones. They are usually free. He'll know what you mean, and will produce three or four pieces of sawn beef leg bone. Cover the bones with water and simmer for at least 2 hours. Remove remaining marrow from the bones and return it to the water. Boil the marrow water until it reduces to 3 to 4 cups. Then add:

1 teaspoon sugar
3 teaspoons black pepper
3 tablespoons butter or margarine
¼ cup white vinegar
3 teaspoons salt (or to taste)
¼ cup minced onion
½ teaspoon cayenne pepper
1 clove minced garlic
1 teaspoon Louisiana hot sauce
2 teaspoons chili powder
1 teaspoon dry mustard
½ teaspoon Wright's smoke sauce
3 teaspoons Worcestershire sauce

Combine all ingredients in a saucepan. Bring to a boil, reduce heat and simmer 10 minutes. Allow sauce to stand at least overnight in refrigerator. Warm sauce before using. This will keep for a month in the refrigerator.

The cayenne pepper is an essential flavoring agent in barbecue recipes. If the sauce is too hot for your taste, delete the Louisiana hot sauce. This basic sauce works equally well on beef, pork and chicken.

The Wood

Good wood is essential to good barbecue, yet in American backyards bad wood and hasty, high-heat cooking are yearly allowed to produce bad barbecue that far outweighs the good.

Charcoal briquets are the least desirable form of barbecue fuel. The neat oval briquets consist of ground, mixed hardwood charcoal reshaped and held together with a cornstarch binder. They burn too fast, fail to impart a hardwood-smoke tang to the meat and when doused with a combustible petroleum distillate invariably make the meat taste faintly of fuel oil.

Any hardwood coals or solid charcoal are better than briquets. The best woods for barbecuing in California and the Pacific Northwest are oak, alder, maple, manzanita, mesquite and the wood of any fruit tree. One of the glories for tourists of Mexican border towns such as Tijuana, Calexico and Nogales is the open-air barbecues where enterprising youngsters cook and sell goat meat grilled over fires of mesquite charcoals.

Solid Mexican charcoal is available in some grocery stores, nurseries and fuel supply stores in Western states. If it is not available near you, try reducing some hardwood firewood coals in the fireplace and simply shovel the coals into the barbecue. Living in the Napa Valley, our family frequently locates old grapevine stumps pulled and discarded by the vineyards. These make excellent heating fuel but even better barbecue coals. The wood turns to coals almost immediately and grills meat with a satisfying wild tang to it.

Consider eliminating charcoal lighter permanently from the barbecue process. It takes just a few minutes longer to build a small fire with paper and kindling. Once burning, this will light solid charcoal or briquets as quickly as the expensive, polluting and ill-tasting lighter fluid.

If you are stuck with briquets, and we all are at times, add a double-handful of water-soaked hickory or alder chips to the fire when the briquets are covered with ash. Hickory and alder chips are available commercially, or you can make your own with a hatchet or axe. Fruitwood, often available from orchards, also does wonders for the taste of barbecue.

During one rainy California winter a few years back, we heated a hillside Napa Valley home with three-foot oak logs from downed timber behind the house. We also had a supply of apple wood from a played-out orchard. The apple chunks turned immediately to coals that fell in bright rings from the logs on the fire. The house smelt faintly of apple perfume. We grilled steaks, hamburger and chops over the apple coals in the fireplace and enjoyed a magnificent flavor that lingers on in family memory.

Grilling with solid charcoal or hardwood coals slows down the cooking process, but this is sure to soothe the soul and give the appetite a natural edge. I still feel a pang of indigestion whenever I recall a scene I witnessed a few years back:

Our family was camping deep in the woods along one of the feeder streams of the upper MacKenzie River east of Eugene, Oregon. On noon of the second day, an out-of-state pickup camper whipped into a campsite downstream. The driver, a squat, fast-moving man, dashed to the rear of the camper, hauled out a portable grill and swiftly turned a half-bag of briquets into it. Doused with lighter fluid, it went up with a loud *whoosh*. The sportsman pulled a rod from the camper and ran to the creek, yelling at his wife to watch the fire. He whipped the creek to a froth, trotting up and down the bank, then dashed back to the grill, threw on some hamburger patties, and ran to the creek again to fish spasmodically. Five minutes later he, his wife and small daughter stood around the grill, wolfing down hamburgers. The sportsman, still running, stowed his rod in the camper, dumped the half-burned briquets in the fire circle and roared off. He had camped, fished, cooked and eaten in less than 45 minutes.

"Ulcer city," laughed our oldest daughter, retrieving the abandoned coals and adding them to our fire.

Equipment

Fish, hamburgers, steaks and lamb shish-kebab grill best over an open charcoal fire. Other meats and cuts of meat, however, benefit from being enclosed by the smoke and receiving heat from all sides. A hooded barbecue, then, is the idea. And, regardless of manufacturers' claims, in barbecue any hood will do, as long as some system of venting allows you control of the draft — and, consequently, the heat and smoke. I have cooked with Weber grills, the Chinese Komodo covered clay barbecue pot, in a rock-lined pit covered with a wooden box, and in a homemade oil drum cut in two lengthwise and fitted with hinges for the top. All worked equally well. In a pinch, you can barbecue great ribs on an inexpensive cast-iron hibachi covered with a roomy cardboard box. Simply cut two slots in the box, one near the bottom and one on top, for a controlled venting system.

Barbecue Meats and Methods

Barbecued Brisket

This recipe, from Texas by way of Southern California, features a simple and natural basting sauce that is also poured over the sliced meat when served.

In a large pot, boil three or four pieces of marrow bones for an hour. Scrape out remaining marrow and remove the bones. Add salt and pepper to taste, ½ teaspoon Wright's smoke sauce and a slash of Louisiana hot sauce. Parboil the brisket (3 to 4 pounds) gently in this broth for 20 to 30 minutes. Then place the brisket on the charcoal grill, sprinkling a double-handful of soaked hickory or alder chips over the ash-covered coals. Keep the heat low and cook covered 30 minutes per side, basting generously with the broth (use an inexpensive, 2-inch paint brush or small barbecue mop). To serve, dip slices of brisket in the heated broth. This brisket is excellent for sandwiches or as a main meat course with barbecued beans.

Note: The skilled pit barbecue cook can control the amount of smoke taste imparted to the meat. For a light taste, leave the top vent of the barbecue hood open. For a heavier smoke taste, open the vent just enough to ensure a steady fire.

Barbecued Ribs

Although beef ribs barbecue well, and may be prepared with this recipe, pork ribs truly provide the finest barbecue texture. The precooking called for in these recipes is the basic key to home barbecue success. Precooking renders off excess fat and takes care of the basic cooking process so that the barbecuing process is a matter of gently tenderizing the meat at low, slow temperatures and letting the blue wood smoke do its magic.

Parboil 3 to 5 pounds of pork ribs in water to cover for 10 minutes (or prebake in a 325° oven for 15 minutes). Place the ribs over a slow charcoal fire (with the draft or damper half-closed) covered with soaked hardwood chips. Cook, covered, 30 minutes per side; during the last 15 minutes, baste generously with the warmed Pit Barbecue Sauce (page 91). Put a dish of the sauce on the table for those who like it poured over their ribs.

Barbecued Fish

The coastal Indians of the Pacific Northwest both steamed and grilled fish. This barbecue method, combining both techniques, produces an herbed, lightly smoked yet juicy fish. My wife is responsible for this recipe and the following one.

4 pounds red snapper, ling cod, striped bass or halibut
1 stick butter or margarine
3 tablespoons grated onion
2 tablespoons minced chives
2 tablespoons minced parsley
2 tablespoons Worcestershire sauce
2 dashes Louisiana hot sauce
Juice of 2 lemons

Salt and pepper the fish. Place on a large sheet of heavy foil. Pour heated sauce over the fish. Seal foil tightly, crimping edges to prevent leaks. Place carefully on charcoal grill and cover with hood. Cook with low heat 20 minutes per side. Then remove fish from foil (reserving the sauce) and place on grill, using a handled grill if fish seems to want to break into pieces. Cook uncovered 10 minutes per side, basting with sauce from the foil wrapper. Pour left-over sauce over fish and serve.

Butterflied Leg of Lamb

This California-Armenian recipe comes originally from the small community of Riverbank, near the Central Valley town of Modesto. Once the complicated marinating process is completed, it is classically simple to cook this meat on the grill.

Have your butcher butterfly a leg of lamb (remove the leg and "aitch" bone). The cut of meat will then lie flat and average 2 inches in thickness.

2 cups burgundy wine
½ cup olive oil
2 tablespoons tarragon vinegar
1 medium onion, finely chopped
1 tablespoon parsley
1 teaspoon basil
1 teaspoon garlic powder (or one clove minced garlic)
½ teaspoon pepper
1 bay leaf, crumbled

Marinate the lamb in this mixture for 48 hours in the refrigerator. Grill to desired doneness on covered barbecue — about 30 minutes per side, basting lightly with the marinade as it cooks.

Barbecued Swordfish or Salmon

The firm texture of swordfish and salmon makes these fish perfect for light charcoal grilling, as coast Indians of the West well knew. Shark, which in the past has been passed off as swordfish in meat markets, is delicious cooked this way. With the inevitable dwindling of ocean fish populations, shark meat will find greater acceptance on American tables. Sand, leopard and lemon sharks, relatively small in size, are excellent eating.

Use swordfish, shark or salmon cut into 2-inch-thick steaks. Grill gently in butter in a frying pan 5 minutes per side. Place the fish on an open charcoal grill with soaked hardwood chips on the coals. Grill 10 minutes per side, basting with lemon-butter sauce. If the hardwood chips flare into flame on the open grill, douse with water.

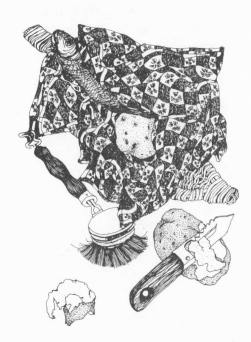

Barbecued Sweet Corn

This recipe is a sanctified tradition in Wisconsin, where the world's most succulent sweet corn is grown. At the annual Wisconsin Day reunions in Los Angeles, barbecued bratwurst and sweet corn become festive communion. Children (and we older children) often peel back the shucks and, holding the stem, eat this corn just like a Popsicle.

Select fresh ears of sweet corn — ideally, picked the same day. Test for proper milk stage by popping a mature grain at the tip of the ear — the white milk should run freely and be thin. Soak the corn ears *at least* 4 hours — overnight is best — in a bucket of salt solution, 1 cup of salt per 2 gallons of water. Place the wet ears directly on the open charcoal grill and cook until done (10 to 20 minutes, depending on heat), turning frequently. Some cooks prefer to strip back the shucks, remove the cornsilk and replace the husks before grilling. It is perfectly proper American sweet corn etiquette to roll the corn ears over a cube of butter. In this household, there is always a plate of ridged sweet corn butter in the refrigerator during the garden corn season.

Barbecued Beans

Surprisingly enough, the relatively short baking time in this recipe produces firm, mealy beans completely penetrated by the sauce — equal in consistency to slow-baked Boston Beans.

½ pound ground beef (may be omitted)
½ pound diced bacon
½ cup chopped onion
1 #2 can B&M beans — or brand equivalent
1 small can green lima beans
1 can red kidney or pinto beans
½ cup chili sauce or catsup
¾ cup brown sugar
1 teaspoon salt
1 teaspoon dry mustard
1 teaspoon vinegar

Fry bacon crisp and drain. Brown ground beef and onion. Combine chili sauce, brown sugar, salt, dry mustard and vinegar. Add ground beef, onion and bacon. Add beans, using liquid from all cans except lima beans. Bake covered in a 2-quart casserole at 350° for 1½ hours.

Sangrita Mix

And finally, for basting the cook and his hungry kibitzing friends gathered around the barbecue grill, California's Mexican-Americans offer the drink of Jalisco known as *Sangrita* (not to be confused with Sangria, a pleasant, innocuous wine and fruit-juice punch). According to my research in clubs, restaurants and cantinas from Tijuana to San Jose, the word loosely translated means something like "the blood of the black widow." With a shot of Sangrita chasing down a shot of tequila, the energy rush becomes a torrent, a river out of its banks. Two Sangritas and you try to make love to the *patron's* wife — or husband. Three Sangritas and you are ready to fight *tigres*.

1 pint orange juice
1 pint tomato juice (if commercial, the justly praised
    Sacramento brand)
Juices of 2 limes
1 10-ounce can of chile salsa, pureed in blender
1 tablespoon Tabasco sauce

Stir ingredients together and chill. Pour out a shot glass of tequila and a shot glass of Sangrita. Take a sip of tequila and chase it with the Sangrita, then chase the fire of the Sangrita with another sip of tequila, and so on. *Adios*.

THE SUMMER GARDEN:
Planting, Preparing and Preserving

The first plantings are done and the gardener now becomes a caretaker, a teaser, a cajoler and a guardian. This chapter focuses on tips for specific crops learned over the years by native gardeners in California and the Pacific Northwest. The preserving instructions and special recipes for using garden produce come from American Indian lore, the country-wise ways of early Western settlers and my own gardening experiences.

For a superbly specific general guide to growing, putting up and cooking garden produce, I recommend the handsome, encyclopedic *Garden-to-Table Cookbook* by Helen Witty and Burton Wolf.

Depending on the size of your garden, the summer work may seen endless, sometimes backbreaking. Yet there is pleasure in working in the heat of a golden summer day, the smells of earth and growing things all around, amidst the variety of greenery and the sight of tomatoes and squash coming into their full color. There's a sense of great adventure in the summer garden, a sense that things are *happening*! Even when the weeding, thinning, watering, pruning, inspecting are done for the time being, the gardener cannot resist stepping onto the back porch or pausing at the kitchen window to observe the object of his or her labors.

Green Beans

Few garden crops are so productive, easy to grow and process as green beans. Thousands of acres of green beans are grown in the rich soil and mild climate of Oregon's Willamette Valley, providing a large percentage of America's canned and frozen green beans.

Green beans are a fairly rapidly maturing, warm-weather crop. The seeds will easily rot in cold, damp soil. Planted in rows two feet apart, thinned to eight-inch spaces in the rows, green beans will flourish in most types of soil with just weekly watering and shallow cultivation. In heavier soils which have a tendency to crust, the ground must be kept moist until the cotyledon (the twin first leaves and the bean itself) emerges; otherwise, it can remain stuck underground, eventually breaking the bean stalk or becoming tasty prey for slugs, snails, wireworms or root maggots. In such cases, gently loosen the soil around the cotyledon with your forefinger and release the plant.

Green beans are especially vulnerable to a leaf rust that is transmitted when the wet plants are disturbed. Always work your beans when they are completely dry.

Most modern, prolific strains of green beans are bred for standard size and standard maturity. In the case of the superb, meaty-tasting and heavily bearing Top Crop variety, for example, all of the plants will bear within the space of a week, and that's about it. To provide a relatively continuous supply of fresh green beans for the table, stagger your plantings. Most bush beans mature in about 55 days; pole beans, such as the time-honored Kentucky Wonder, mature in 60 to 70 days, so Kentucky Wonder beans planted along a fence, trellis, or in corn, will extend the fresh bean season considerably, since Kentucky Wonders will bear for a month in hot climates (up until frost in milder summer climates).

Green beans also flourish as a fall crop, further extending the bearing season. Yellow, crisp and tender wax beans like the cooler fall nighttime temperatures. In California and the Pacific Northwest a fall crop may be planted any time between August 1st and 15th.

Preparing and Preserving   Green beans are easily processed whole, snapped, or Frenched (cut into julienne strips — a green bean Frencher is available through the Burpee catalog). Many persons, myself included, consider the flavor of frozen green beans inferior to that of canned ones. If canned, the beans must be processed in a pressure cooker, since they are nonacid.

Another extremely simple, and picturesque, method of preserving green beans is to use the southwestern American Indian method of drying them, making strings of "leather britches" beans, as American settlers called them (dried beans look exactly like leather britches). Simply string the beans, flat-wise, with a needle and stout thread. Hang three-foot-long bunches of them in a sunny window or outdoor location (bringing them in at night). In about two months, they will be dried to a tough and leathery texture and may be stored all winter in air-tight containers such as gallon jars or may be left hanging in a dry place until used. Reconstituted and well-cooked, they make a nourishing and delicious vegetable dish.

Settlers moving West found many variations on the recipe given here among Indian tribes from Virginia to Arizona to Oregon:

Cooking Leather Britches Beans

1 pound dried green beans
2 quarts water
¼ pound salt pork, bacon or hamhock, diced
2 teaspoons salt
¼ teaspoon fresh ground pepper

Soak the beans overnight (or at least 2 hours) in the water. Add the salt pork, salt and pepper. Bring to a boil, then simmer gently for 3 hours, stirring occasionally. Add water to cover if necessary. The broth is a superb "pot likker" and should be sopped up with skillet cornbread.

Lima Beans

Another New World vegetable long cultivated by American Indians, lima beans are grown like green beans with certain small exceptions. Limas germinate in even warmer soil than green beans, so should be planted after May 1st in most California and Pacific Northwest locations. They are slower to mature, seeming to wait around for hot weather to flourish (about 75 days, depending on the variety). The large, luxuriant Fordhook variety should be thinned to one foot apart in the row to make room for the two-foot-tall plants. Side-dressing with manure when the plants first bloom definitely increases the productivity of limas.

Limas were originally a pole bean, and pole varieties still yield much more heavily and over a longer period than the bush beans but take longer to mature (up to 100 days for the Southern "butterbean" varieties). Limas also produce over a longer period of time than green beans. Fresh lima beans from one crop may grace the kitchen table for several weeks at a time.

Preparing and Preserving   Lima beans seem to be created for freezing, but they may be pressure canned (at considerable loss in flavor) and, of course, dried right on the vines (which are then pulled, dried more thoroughly a day or two in the sun, and threshed or shelled out; if dried beans are to be stored, put them in the freezer for at least one hour to kill weevil larvae).

There may be no finer fate for a lima than to be combined with fresh garden corn in succotash, another uniquely American garden meal inherited from the Indians. The word is apparently a garbled English transliteration of an East Coast Indian name. The dried succotash recipe below was a winter vegetable staple for ages in American Indian stewpots.

Garden Succotash

5 ears corn
2 cups fresh lima beans
¼ pound diced bacon
1 small onion
⅓ cup chopped green pepper (or red bell pepper)
1 tablespoon butter or margarine

Boil corn 10 minutes and cut from cob into a 2-quart saucepan, salting lightly. Boil lima beans separately for 10 minutes in lightly salted water and add to corn. Fry diced bacon in skillet until crisp; remove with slotted spoon and drain. Sauté diced onions and peppers in 2 tablespoons grease until golden; add to corn and lima beans along with ½ cup water and the butter. Simmer gently, covered, for 15 minutes. During the last 3 minutes, add the cream. For interesting herb variations, dust lightly with paprika or add 1 teaspoon crumbled, dried savory to the mixture before final cooking. Crumble the crisp bacon over the dish before serving it.

Note: To prepare with frozen vegetables, mix 2 cups frozen corn and 2 cups frozen lima beans, add the sautéed onion and peppers and cook all for 20 minutes.

Dried-Corn-and-Lima Succotash

1 cup dried corn
1 cup dried lima beans

Soak the corn and limas separately overnight in water to cover. Drain and simmer corn and limas together for 1 hour in water to cover and salt to taste. Continue as in the Garden Succotash, cooking all for 20 minutes. A hearty flavor that brightens midwinter days with a tang of the sweet summer earth.

Sweet Corn

Anyone who has ever tasted the sweet, juicy perfection of sweet corn grown in the American Corn Belt (it is the world's finest) knows how suitable the humid summers and warm nights of the Midwest must be for that delicacy. However, with irrigation and careful culture we can grow sweet corn close to that standard of excellence.

The basic problem with growing sweet corn is space. A family-sized plot requires at least 20 feet by 20 feet of garden. However, pumpkins may be grown in the corn, and Kentucky Wonder beans may be planted in the rows to climb the stalks, thus using the required space more intensively.

To ensure a summer-long supply instead of a glut of simultaneously maturing ears, stagger plantings of one variety at two-week intervals; or, better yet, plant three differently maturing (and tasting) varieties at once — an early, a middle and a late-season corn.

I am quite disenchanted with the widely popular Golden Bantam variety. It seems to have been bred for quantity, not quality, and its kernels, though plump, are tough. Many country sweet corn fanciers derisively call it "horse corn." A superb short-stalked early corn (53 days) is Early Sunglow. Excellent middle-season varieties (70 days) are Illini Xtra Sweet, Iochief and the superlatively tender Butter and Cream (mixed yellow and white grains). My own favorite varieties are the late-season (90 days) long-eared yet tender Silver Queen and Country Gentleman (or Shoe Peg, so named for the random arrangement of the kernels). Silver Queen also has the advantage of growing tight ears, the shucks of which are practically impenetrable to corn earworms (though in general the damage to corn ears done by this pest is more aesthetic than practical).

Sweet corn must be planted in short blocks rather than in a few long rows, since wind has to do its work in spreading the pollen from the tassels of one plant to the stalks and corn ears of another. Plants must be thinned to at least one foot apart in rows or you will get lush foliage instead of corn ears. Also, sweet corn is a greedy feeder, requiring ample water and fertilizer.

As with lima beans, it takes a practiced eye and sensitive fingers to detect the mature and ripe product. Sweet corn ears are mature when the corn silks just begin to darken and when the ear feels full to the touch. To double-check a doubtful ear, gently pull back a strip of the shuck and look for full grains; carefully replace the shuck if the ear is not yet ready.

Preparing and Preserving   There is a country adage that when corn is picked a pot of water must be at the boil — and the sun must never set on a shucked ear. Freshness is essential because the corn sugar begins immediately to turn to starch when the ear is plucked.

In cooking sweet corn, add a few drops of milk or a few green shucks to the boiling water. This seems to keep the corn tender and enhance the natural flavor.

Dried corn shucks will keep almost indefinitely for use as tamale wrappers (see page 55). My own family always cuts dried cornstalks and ties them into shocks for Halloween doorway decorations; indeed, we often leave the shocks standing most of the winter as a reminder of summer's bounty.

Skillet Corn

Many a farm child in the Pacific Northwest remembers this quick sweet-corn dish of Indian origin.

4 strips diced bacon
6 ears sweet corn
4 chopped green onions
1 tablespoon fresh dill, if available
1 tablespoon minced parsley
½ teaspoon salt
Pepper to taste
1½ cups water

Boil sweet corn in water to cover 10 minutes. Fry diced bacon just until crisp. Cut kernels from corn cobs into a bowl, scraping off pulp and milk also. Add corn to bacon and drippings; stir in onions, dill, parsley, salt and pepper. Stir and sauté for 10 minutes. Add water, cover and simmer for ½ hour.

Dried Corn

Freezing and canning are the best-tasting methods of preserving sweet corn, in that order. Small ears may be blanched and frozen whole with surprisingly little loss in quality. Before the days of processing, however, dried corn was a staple of American Indian and settler's diets.

The process is quite simple. Select, pick and shuck mature ears of sweet corn. Place them in the sun on a clean board. If flies are a problem, cover with window screen or cheesecloth. Bring the corn indoors at night to avoid dew. In about a week, the ears will have dried enough for the grains to be shriveled. Shell the grains onto cookie sheets or a piece of plywood and return to the sun. Depending on the weather, the grains will take another week to dry. When dry and hard, store in a dry place in airtight containers. Reconstitute by soaking in water to cover overnight.

Tomatoes

Consider the patient, abiding tomato. Gardeners throughout the United States become furiously partisan about the best way to stake, prune, fertilize and cultivate tomatoes. (See pages 33-35 for this gardener's ideas on the subject). These hardy plants seem to endure the extremes of smothering care and neglect and, if tended prudently, will continue sending out a profusion of new shoots and blossoms in the lower elevations of California and the Pacific Northwest until the first November frosts.

My family simply luxuriates in tomatoes from June through November, enjoying a steady procession of tomatoes fried, tomatoes stuffed (with tuna salad, with chopped zucchini, with bread crumbs, with yellow crookneck squash), tomatoes sliced (and cottage cheese), tomato juice, sauce and relish, and sun-warmed tomatoes eaten out of hand with a salt shaker handy.

Fried Green Tomatoes

Some folks are startled by the idea, but those who grew up in garden and country ways just come naturally to fried green tomatoes. That first, mellow-tart taste, however, will convert anybody. This is an excellent substitute for potatoes at dinner and goes naturally with eggs at breakfast.

Slice tomatoes ½ inch thick — do not peel or core. Drain between folded paper toweling until relatively dry. Dredge slices in flour that has been seasoned with salt and pepper. Let stand on paper toweling for about 15 minutes for coating to set. Sauté until lightly browned in butter or bacon drippings. Serve on a hot platter.

Herbed Fried Green Tomatoes

A slightly more elaborate version, breaded and cooked something like wienerschnitzel.

2 pounds green tomatoes, sliced and dried (see Fried Green Tomatoes)
4 eggs
1 cup flour
¾ cup water
¼ cup minced fresh basil or chives
1 tablespoon salt
Pepper to taste

Make a batter by beating eggs well, then mixing in flour, water, minced herbs, salt and pepper. Dip the tomato slices in the batter and brown on both sides in a skillet containing ⅓ cup butter or bacon drippings. Serve on a preheated platter.

Basic Tomato Sauce

A family recipe developed over the years, this tomato sauce can go virtually anywhere — into casseroles, Mexican dishes and with pasta. It is akin to a *marinara* sauce and, with mushrooms added, makes a fine spaghetti sauce as is. We convert at least 30 pints of garden tomatoes each year into this sauce, and it never lasts until the next tomato season. Any variety of tomato may be used, but the mealy San Marzano and Roma plum tomatoes work best. Try planting a few of these hardy, productive plants as a source for sauce and tomato paste, as a thickener for tomato juice, and for salads. This recipe makes about 8 pints, but may be halved successfully.

```
10 pounds (about 2 dozen medium) ripe tomatoes
 2 medium onions, chopped
 8 cloves of garlic, chopped fine
⅔ cup olive or salad oil
 2 green peppers, seeded and chopped
 3 teaspoons salt
1½ teaspoons pepper
 2 tablespoons dried, crushed oregano
1½ teaspoons crumbled rosemary leaves
 1 teaspoon fresh chopped basil, or ½ teaspoon dry basil
 2 teaspoons paprika
About 3 cups dry red wine
```

Cook onions and garlic in olive oil in a large frying pan until golden, stirring occasionally. Cook *slowly*. Peel tomatoes by dipping into boiling water for 1 minute, then immediately plunging into cold water. Skins will slip off easily. Cut tomatoes into quarters and place in a kettle. Bring tomatoes, sautéed onions and garlic and chopped peppers to a boil and simmer 15 minutes, stirring and breaking up larger chunks of tomatoes. When tomatoes are soft, run through a food mill, discarding seeds and fiber left behind. Return to the fire, add all the other ingredients and simmer slowly, stirring occasionally, about 1 hour or until desired tomato-sauce thickness is achieved. Ladle into hot, sterilized jars and process for 15 minutes in a boiling-water bath. This sauce also freezes well.

Wheeler Chili Sauce

Probably no preserved food is so intimately associated with country childhood as homemade chili sauce. Time and again, when conversation comes around to chili sauce, I've observed bursts of hearty nostalgia about elderly aunts, parents or grandparents who made their own. Wendy Wheeler, the artist-illustrator of this book, dug into her files and produced her father's New York recipe, which the Wheeler children grew up on. Having made it in large amounts, I can tell you that this is the genuine article.

12 large ripe tomatoes, peeled and chopped
 2 medium onions, chopped fine
 2 green or red sweet peppers, chopped
 1 teaspoon cinnamon
 1 teaspoon salt
 ½ cup sugar

Peel tomatoes as for Basic Tomato Sauce. Place all ingredients in a large kettle and simmer gently for about 2 hours or until desired chili-sauce thickness is reached. Stir occasionally. Ladle into hot, sterilized jars. To store any length of time, process in boiling water, 20 minutes for quarts, 15 minutes for pints.

California Chili Sauce

This early Spanish-American chili sauce begins like the recipe above but then quickly becomes the green-chili *salsa* so fundamental to good Mexican cookery. It is well worth putting up because of its versatility as a dinner-table seasoning, as base for an appetizer dip and as the starting point for homemade sauces for Enchiladas, Tamales (page 55) and Huevos Rancheros (page 61).

Follow the recipe in Wheeler Chili Sauce, omitting the cinnamon. Add 2 to 4 diced and seeded hot green chiles (Fresno or jalapeño), 1 teaspoon celery seed and 2 tablespoons chili powder. For storing any length of time, process as for Wheeler Chili Sauce.

Tomato Juice

This is the perfect way to use overripe, blemished and surplus tomatoes. The method is simplicity itself, and you may create zesty flavors to suit your family's palate by a judicious use of onion and celery salt added before the juice goes into the jars.

Peel and quarter tomatoes using the boiling-water dip method described for Basic Tomato Sauce (page 122). In a kettle, bring tomatoes to a boil and simmer just until they are cooked and softened (about 15 minutes). To each quart of tomatoes, add 1 tablespoon sugar and 1 teaspoon salt (adjust to taste before putting juice into jars). Run tomatoes and juice through a food mill, discarding seeds and coarse pulp. Add onion and/or celery salt to taste, ladle into hot, sterilized jars. Process 10 minutes in a boiling water bath.

Note: A few Roma or San Marzano paste tomatoes will give nice body to juice made from regular tomatoes.

Cucumbers and Pickles

Cucumbers   In working among his or her plants, the gardener soon develops a finely tuned sense of individual personality in garden species. Zucchini plants are shamelessly boisterous in their abundance, gross, even slightly obscene in their rapid, rough growth. Cucumbers, on the other hand, are the coy and shy creatures of the garden. They will wither, balk at growing, or not pollinate evenly unless watered with careful regularity. Too much shade and they get spindly; too much hot sun and they turn droopy and limp. Too much moisture and the cucumbers swell, turn soft and rot easily. And if cucumbers aren't picked regularly the vine stops setting on new fruit.

But if all the cucumber's demands are met, and if well-rotted manure is dug into the seedbed, it will respond with bumper crops all summer long. Six climbing cucumber plants furnish our family with a summer's supply of slicing, pickling and relish cucumbers. In fact, during pickling season many years ago my small daughters made summer pin money in the neighborhood by selling wagons-full of dark green cucumbers.

For all-around use, pickling cucumbers such as the Liberty Hybrid, Ohio Pickler and Wisconsin SMR are the best. The fruit may be picked at the desired size for gherkins, small sweet pickles, or dill pickles — and larger fruit are perfect for slicing fresh.

Cucumbers love to climb and will produce cleaner, straighter fruit when allowed to do so. Wooden trellises or string netting are best for this purpose, since metal fencing heated by the sun will burn the sensitive clinging tendrils. Cucumbers will tolerate shade during part of the day. Just remember to water them well and regularly, and methodically pick all mature fruit (although one or two always seem to remain hidden and are discovered only later, swollen huge and pale yellow).

Pickles   Many folks who do not garden or preserve food extensively still take pride in putting up sparkling jars of homemade pickles and relishes, giving their dinner tables that individual touch that reflects human concern. The pickle and relish recipes here are part of a traceable 200-year family tradition. (I am probably the only male in the line of descent to collect and use them.)

"Best Dill Pickles Ever"

This recipe, of German origin, was given to me by Josephine Strid, of Wells, Minnesota. It is a simple and absolutely foolproof method that produces firm, crisp dills and has eliminated the messy, unpredictable crock-fermenting method from my pickle repertory forever.

For the *brine,* bring 7 cups water, 5 cups cider vinegar, 1 cup kosher or pickling (noniodized) salt to a boil.

Carefully wash fresh dill-sized pickles and pack loosely in a jar. Fill jar to top with boiling water and let stand until cool. Drain off water. To each jar add ⅛ teaspoon powdered dill or two washed grape leaves (these contain alum) and place a large sprig of fresh dill on top. Fill with hot pickling brine (at boiling point) and seal. Pickles will remain firm and clear. Ready to eat in about 2 weeks.

The amount of liquid given here will fill about 6 quart jars. Any left-over brine can be stored in a glass jar in the refrigerator and may be heated up and used later. For taste variations, add 1 tablespoon mixed pickling spices to the brine before heating.

For kosher dills, place 1 peeled clove of garlic and 1 small dried hot pepper in each jar before adding brine.

Bread and Butter Pickles

My aunt, Irene Morris, of Kirksville, Missouri, first acquainted me with this pickle method, which appears to be the basic, universal bread and butter pickle recipe in America.

5 pounds sliced pickling cucumbers
3 large onions, sliced thin
2 green or red bell peppers, chopped or sliced in strips
2 cloves garlic, minced
⅓ cup salt (plain or kosher)
1 teaspoon powdered alum
5 cups sugar
3 cups cider vinegar
1 teaspoon turmeric (or marigold petals)
2 teaspoons celery seed
2 tablespoons mustard seed
Ice cubes

Mix cucumbers, onions, peppers and garlic. Add the salt and alum. Cover the surface with ice cubes and let stand in a mixing bowl for 3 hours, stirring occasionally. Add ice cubes as needed to keep the pickles covered completely. Drain off the liquid. Combine sugar, vinegar and spices. Put all ingredients in a stainless steel, glass or enamel pot and mix. Boil at least 3 minutes. Pour pickles and liquid into sterilized jars and seal. Makes about 6 pints. May be eaten in a week, but will continue to improve in flavor throughout the first month.

Sweet Relish

8 large ripe cucumbers (or 10 pickling cucumbers)
¼ cup pickling salt
4 sweet red peppers, seeded and cored
4 large onions, quartered
1½ tablespoons celery seed
1½ tablespoons mustard seed
2½ cups sugar
1½ cups white vinegar

Peel and slice cucumbers. Place in a stainless steel, crockery or glass bowl. Add salt and mix well; cover and let stand in refrigerator overnight. Drain. Put cucumbers, peppers and onion through food chopper, using coarse blade. Bring the mixture to a boil in a kettle after mixing with other ingredients. Simmer, uncovered, 30 minutes, stirring off and on. Ladle into hot, sterilized jars and seal immediately.

Piccalilli

Jars of colorful, zesty piccalilli are the mark of the productive gardener. In midsummer, when everything in the garden is swelling and plumping into crowded maturity, piccalilli is an excellent way to use up the dismayingly bountiful baskets of cabbages, peppers and tomatoes.

```
  2 sweet red peppers, chopped
  2 green peppers, chopped
  6 green tomatoes (4 cups), chopped
  1 cup chopped celery
  2 large onions, chopped
  1 small head cabbage, chopped
  ½ cup coarse (noniodized) salt
  3 cups cider vinegar
  1 teaspoon dry mustard
2¼ cups brown sugar
  1 teaspoon turmeric (or marigold petals)
```

Place peppers, tomatoes, celery, onion and cabbage in layers in a stainless steel, crockery or glass bowl, sprinkling each layer with salt. Let stand, covered, at room temperature overnight. Drain. Put mixture in a large kettle and add remaining ingredients. Bring to a boil and simmer, uncovered, 15 to 20 minutes, stirring frequently. Ladle into hot, sterilized pint jars and seal. Process 5 minutes in boiling-water bath. Makes 5 to 6 pints.

Jams and Jellies:
Captured Sunshine

If sunshine has a flavor, it is that bright, warm, unmistakably wild taste that is caught in the flavor of homemade jams and jellies made from foraged blackberries, elderberries, dewberries, salmon and olallieberries. We have not bought a jar of commercially made jam or jelly in over fifteen years, and only rarely do we buy fruit for preserving. California, Oregon and Washington roadsides, woods, streambanks and vacant lots are lush with the fruits mentioned above. Moreover, berrying expeditions are a family outing for us, and one the youngsters especially enjoy — an exciting hunt for treasure.

We have occasionally encountered an over-civilized hesitancy in some people to forage for nature's foods. If it's free, they seem to want to say, or growing alongside a road, there must be something wrong with it. For most folks, though, it takes no more than a taste of the preserves (we've been known to make special Christmas gifts to the skeptics among our friends) to convert them. Doubt dissolves into delighted amazement at the unforgettably robust tang of the wild fruit.

The comprehensive jam-and-jelly-making instructions that come with each box of Sure-Jell pectin can guide even the beginner in preparing the results of a day's berrying. Here are, in addition, some country tips to good jam and jelly making: For jam from seedy berries such as blackberries and raspberries, run half the recipe through the food mill to remove excess seeds. Mildly-flavored, low-acid berries such as blueberries, elderberries and salmonberries pick up flavor and a subtle tartness from the addition of the juice of one lemon before processing.

Sauerkraut

For a small family, several five-pound to eight-pound garden cabbage heads can be an embarrassment of riches. A whole bowl of fresh cabbage slaw needs only a quarter of one large head. The answer: a winter's supply of fresh and tangy, naturally fermented sauerkraut. It is the easiest of all garden vegetables to put up. And it is delicious. "Oh boy," my German father used to exclaim over a bowl of sauerkraut and spare ribs, rubbing his hands, "German honey!"

I never fail to recall, as I shred big, firm heads of Flat Dutch cabbage each summer, and pack quart jars with kraut-to-be, my father's introduction to my mother's Missouri hill-country family.

It was during the Depression, and my father and mother had returned to Missouri from California for a family visit. They were staying with Uncle Dude and Aunt Mattie, my mother's sister, who, poor but proud and very independent, were raising a family of eight children by working a leased 160-acre farm. During the summer, Dude and his older boys worked in the fields from dawn to dusk. The family raised and preserved practically all its food, supplementing the meat portion of its diet with fresh game, which the younger children hunted for the table.

In Missouri farm fashion, Dude and his boys wore big, heavy, high-topped shoes, without socks, when working outdoors. Aged in mud and manure, these primeval brogans, looking as stiff and crude as if they had been hewn from wood, were not particularly welcome in the farmhouse. So the men would usually leave their shoes ranked in rows on the back porch and pad about the house in sock feet.

On the second night of my parents' visit that distant August, my father got up in the middle of the night to visit the outhouse. Passing the silent row of gaping shoes, he was almost sent to his knees by a rank and powerful smell that blanketed the porch. Easing back into bed, his errand complete, he had to register a complaint with his semi-awake wife.

"They're good people, your family, but I wish to God Dude and those boys would wash their feet once in a while!"

Which hurt my mother a bit, for although her large family was farm poor, they were fastidious in both dress and hygiene.

Vindication came the next morning. After breakfast the men headed out to the creek-bottom with the mule teams to put up the clover and timothy hay, and Mattie and her girls went to the back porch and began carrying in two-dozen jars of fully fermented sauerkraut for hot-bath processing and putting by. The kitchen filled, much to my father's embarrassment, with that same rank and powerful stench. Father felt honor-bound to confess his unjust suspicions of the night before — which infinitely delighted Uncle Dude and his boys that evening. You can imagine the teasing variations on the story whenever my father encounters sauerkraut during a visit to any member of my mother's family.

It was also in the hills of northern Missouri that I encountered a popular, regularly served sauerkraut dish — called "sweet kraut" — I've seen nowhere else. Apparently its origins are Pennsylvania-Dutch, but I have never overcome my outraged sense of decorum enough to enjoy the recipe. To make it, sauerkraut is gently simmered in water in a large iron skillet until just tender, then a cup of sugar is stirred into the mixture, which is simmered a little longer. Sweet kraut was a favorite dish of my country cousins, aunts and uncles.

Making Kraut

For making large quantities of sauerkraut, a kraut shredder is very handy. Many seed catalogs (Henry Field's and Burpee's, to name two) list them. The implement fits across a crock or large bowl and reduces a head of cabbage to shredded kraut very quickly. For putting up a few heads of cabbage, however, the shredding is easily done with a large, sharp butcher knife. About two pounds of cabbage will fill a quart jar.

Quarter and core each head of cabbage and shred fine. Pack the cabbage into sterilized pint or quart jars. Pack half-full, then sprinkle in 1 teaspoon salt. Continue packing with cabbage up to the shoulder of the jar, then sprinkle in another teaspoon salt. Fill to just under the brim with cold water. Place lids on the jars, but adjust very loosely. Let sit at room temperature to ferment for 9 to 10 days. Then skim off any scum that rises to the top and adjust water to leave about 1½ inches head space. Screw lids down tight and process in boiling water to store, 15 minutes for pints, 20 minutes for quarts. Count processing time as soon as jars are placed in vigorously boiling water.

Cooking Sauerkraut

There are several simple ways to soften the sharp taste of fresh sauerkraut, which bothers some folks. When cooking, drain the original fluid — or part of it, depending on your taste — and replace with water. Add one teaspoon of caraway seed to simmering kraut. Peel, core, and cut up two small tart apples and cook with the kraut. Any pork — fresh shoulder, pork steaks, pork chops or, best of all, ribs — has a natural affinity with sauerkraut. The pork juice softens both the taste and texture of fresh sauerkraut.

Then there is, of course, that uniquely American, German-Midwestern delicacy, the Reuben sandwich, made with kraut. A Reuben is made like a grilled cheese sandwich, except the filling is cooked kraut, slices of corned beef and a slice of brick, Monterey Jack or Swiss cheese.

Making Beer

Beer making and wine and cheese making (which will be covered in later chapters) stand apart from most of the cooking and preserving methods set down in this book. First, they involve gathering some special equipment. Much of it you can make or improvise yourself, and many items can be found used at garage sales or second-hand stores or are readily available at specialty shops. Second, making beer, wine or cheese at home requires an investment of time and thought into some fairly exacting — though relatively simple — processes. The effort, however, will be repaid handsomely, and once the equipment is gathered, the first-timer feels a great surge of confidence and an eagerness to get underway.

The time spent making your own beer (or anything, for that matter) is a reflective time, perhaps a corner of privacy in an otherwise crowded life. It will give you the satisfaction of time well used, for in partnership with nature's processes, you will have enlarged your capabilities and your experience of life. In the long run, the most important reward is not just the product itself (which will probably be outstanding) or the fact that you've trimmed your grocery or beverage bill (which you will) but that you've done something yourself. And if it's beer you've made, the tangible expression of your self-reliance will be a wholesome, rich and clear-tasting beer capable of a robust flavor that is not found in any of the overstandardized American brands.

Prohibition, unfortunately, gave home beer making a bad name in this country. Most people have memories of quickly made home brew exploding in bottles in the cellar or of green, half-fermented liquid full of bread yeast that gave gas pains and the green-apple quickstep. The beer you'll make is of another class altogether.

The process given here produces premium quality steam beer, German lager and British ale at a price of about $2 a case, as opposed to $15 a case for those imported items. It is not home brew but slowly aged, long-fermented (lagered, to use the technical word borrowed from the German) beer. Unlike the other gardening, gathering, preserving and cooking arts given here, which I have collected and learned from earlier generations, this home brewing method is one that I have perfected myself after twenty years of experimenting, consulting German brewing books and hanging around small regional breweries pestering braumeisters and the help with questions.

Like the chicken and the egg, it is difficult to tell whether the coarsening of American beer taste or the economizing motives of the big breweries is responsible for the thin, pale, chemicalized malt beverage that today goes under the labels of America's best-selling beers. (Even the big breweries themselves, in company literature, refer to their product as "malt beverage" rather than beer.)

By German law, all beer sold in Germany may contain only four ingredients besides water: malt, hops, yeast and salt. Most American beer uses rice and corn grits along with some malt. This produces a paler, more tasteless beer but saves the brewers an enormous amount of money. Also, rather than charge the beer with carbon dioxide through natural fermentation, American brewers draw off the carbon dioxide produced during fermentation and later recharge the bottled beer. They pasteurize it (except for Coors and a few small regional breweries), add coloring, yeast conditioners and chemicals to improve the head.

Up until twenty years ago one of the pleasures of sampling the diversity of regional American foods was enjoying the distinctive tastes of beers produced in hundreds of small breweries scattered around the country, most established in the 19th century by German, Polish and Czech immigrants. Today, most of these breweries have gone under or have been assimilated by the five major breweries. However, good local beer may still be found produced in upper New York state, Pennsylvania and Wisconsin. And on the West Coast, both the Anchor Steam Brewery in San Francisco and the family-owned Blitz-Weinhard Brewery in Oregon are enjoying a

renaissance of popularity as beer drinkers seek an honest
malt product they can drink and even bite down on. In
Wisconsin, the Heileman Brewery in La Crosse still
produces perhaps the finest American beer in Heileman's
Special Export, a robust, well-hopped German beer.
Heileman's has not only avoided corporate takeover by the
big breweries but has recently expanded its operations by
purchasing the Rainier Brewery in Seattle. Interestingly
enough, Heileman's, Olympia, Budweiser and Shaefer are
the only four American breweries who carbonate their beer
by a natural, ages-old process called *krausening,* which
involves infusing fermenting batches of beer with small
amounts of fresh-ferment beer to kick up the carbonation.

Making beer, like making wine, is an essentially
simple process that takes a very modest investment of
equipment. As in wine making, however, the simplicity of
the process is complicated by the necessity for developing a
subtle judgment of yeast action and yeast-enhancing
temperatures. Beer-making equipment, like that for
making wine, must also be kept scrupulously clean. Any
residues of yeasts or sugars will invariably spoil a batch of
beer. But if the correct temperatures are maintained, and
the equipment is thoroughly sterilized, practically nothing
else can go wrong with a batch of beer.

The recipes here are for lager beer, ale and pilsner
beer. Technically, the lager beer process produces what is
called "steam" beer, which has nothing to do with steam. It

is merely lager beer which is fermented at room temperatures rather than at the controlled 34°-40° F required for true lager beer. For lager beer, do your secondary fermentation in an old refrigerator with the shelves removed to accommodate a five-gallon carboy. This cooler temperature slows down the secondary fermentation to about a month or six weeks, but it is the mellowest of home-brewed beers, and your hydrometer will accurately tell you when it is time to bottle.

Equipment

Primary fermenter — an 8-gallon crock (no smaller), or a
    clean plastic trash basket
5-gallon glass water bottle (carboy)
Large enamel or stainless steel kettle
Hydrometer and jar
Syphon hose
Bottle capper
Crown caps
2½ cases returnable beer bottles (or 20 returnable quart
    beer bottles)
Fermentation lock

Lager Beer

1 3-pound can Blue Ribbon malt (the pale, hopped variety).
Other brands, such as John Bull, are also available in
wine and beer supply stores. The Canadian barley
malts are excellent.
5 gallons water
3 pounds sugar (preferably corn sugar)
1 teaspoon citric acid (or juice of one lemon)
2 teaspoons salt
1 teaspoon yeast energizer
½ teaspoon Knox gelatin
1 teaspoon ascorbic acid
Lager beer yeast

     1. Pour malt syrup into 1 gallon hot water in large
stainless steel or enamel kettle. Bring to just under a boil,
stirring occasionally, to make "wort."
     2. Put sugar (less 2 cups, which will be added later
during bottling), salt and citric acid in primary fermenter.
     3. Pour hot wort (Step 1) into primary fermenter and
stir to dissolve sugar. Add 4 gallons water.
     4. When temperature of wort is 65°, gently stir in 1
package lager beer yeast. Cover fermenter with plastic
sheet and tie down. Starting specific gravity should be 1.035
to 1.040. (Instructions for measuring specific gravity will
come with your hydrometer.)

5. In 5 to 6 days, when specific gravity is 1.010, syphon into carboy, leaving dead yeast deposit on the bottom in primary fermenter. Add yeast energizer. Add "finings" (½ teaspoon Knox gelatin dissolved for 15 minutes in ½ cup water, brought to a boil for 3 minutes, then allowed to cool to room temperature — this will "clarify" the wort). Attach fermentation lock.

6. Ferment in a cool place (55° to 65° F) for approximately 2 weeks or until specific gravity is 1.000.

7. Syphon beer into primary fermenter leaving yeast residue on the bottom of the carboy (this makes excellent bread yeast). Dissolve remaining 2 cups of sugar in a small amount of beer. Gently stir this syrup and 1 teaspoon ascorbic acid into beer.

8. Syphon into bottles and cap with crown caps.

9. Store for 2 weeks, preferably at a steady temperature of 60°– 70° F. Chill well and serve.

Ale

Use the same recipe but substitute ale yeast for lager yeast and stir daily. In all but definitely hard-water areas, add 2 ounces gypsum or ½ teaspoon Epsom salts to the water to harden it.

Pilsner Beer

Use the lager beer recipe, but use 2 3-pound cans of hopped malt syrup. Starting specific gravity will be approximately 1.045 to 1.050. This will be a robust, full-bodied, European-type beer.

Beer-Making Tips

1. The fermentation times given here are approximate; fluctuations in temperature (to be avoided if possible) and the unpredictable nature of yeasts will speed up or slow down both the primary and secondary fermentation. The green, cidery, sweetish taste of "home brew" is due to the fact that it goes directly into the bottle from primary fermentation without any aging. Also, most "home brew" is made with bread yeast, which is definitely not suitable for beer.

2. Lager yeast is a "bottom acting" yeast which works best at cool temperatures. Ale yeast is a "top acting" yeast which works best at temperatures of 55°– 70° F. The home beer maker can easily notice the different actions of the two yeasts. I generally use ale yeast for beer making in warm weather and lager yeast in cold weather.

3. Blue Ribbon Malt Syrup is available in many grocery stores. All the ingredients listed here are becoming more and more available in wine and beer supply stores — especially now that the United States government and most states have legalized beer making. (At the repeal of Prohibition, the pressures of Italian families on legislators ensured a law allowing the head of a household to make 200 gallons of wine a year; however, no one looked out for the interests of home beer makers. To my knowledge, though, the federal Alcohol Tax Unit has never prosecuted anyone for home brewing.)

Heading liquids, expensive fining gelatins and packaged hops are available in beer supply stores but are not really necessary for making high quality beer. If, however, you wish a well-hopped beer, you can buy unhopped malt and add two ounces Cluster or Brewer's Gold Hops (which come in a cake), broken up and tied in a cheesecloth bag. Add this to the hot wort and also suspend it in the primary fermenter. Or, you may use hopped malt syrup and put one-half ounce of Kent Finishing Hops in a cheesecloth bag and hang it in the wort in the primary fermenter.

4. Always wash and sterilize equipment thoroughly. Rinse all equipment and bottles with a solution of two ounces of metabisulphite in one gallon of water.

5. The two cups of sugar mixed into the beer at bottling time renews fermentation to produce natural carbonation. This process takes from ten days to two weeks in the bottle; the beer is then mellow, well-aged and ready.

6. There will be a normal, thin film of yeast in the bottom of each beer bottle. When pouring the beer, decant all of the bottle at once, tilting the bottle gently to avoid "glugging" and stirring up the yeast sediment. Leave about one-half inch of beer in the bottle. Rinse bottles immediately after pouring; once the yeast sediment dries, it is difficult to remove. Actually, the yeast sediment is good for you, but some people dislike the yeasty taste.

7. Beer improves with age in the bottle if stored in a cool place, though after six months it begins to lose quality.

8. German breweries have used and maintained a specific strain of lager yeast for over 900 years. Once you have purchased lager or ale yeast you, too, can maintain a continuous supply by a method similar to saving sourdough bread starter. After syphoning beer into bottles, pour off at least a cup of the yeast residue in the fermenter and store it in the refrigerator in a glass jar or crock with a tight lid. Add at least one-half cup of this yeast culture to your next batch of beer instead of the packaged yeast. It will produce a quick, vigorous ferment.

9. "Stuck" fermentation means the wort either does not begin to ferment at all or goes dead midway in the process. This is rare and is due to bad yeast, too high an initial fermentation temperature or unsterilized equipment. In twenty years of beer making, the writer has suffered only one stuck batch, a complicated oatmeal stout that wasn't very good even after achieving a successful batch. There are ways of getting a stuck ferment going again by adding a fresh infusion of yeast, but the quality of the beer, which depends heavily on a vigorous, continuous ferment, will suffer. The best thing to do is throw out a stuck batch of wort and start over.

10. The chemical reaction that makes beer is another of nature's simple, straightforward miracles. Yeast works on sugar to produce carbon dioxide and alcohol. Malt provides sugar, color and flavor. Hops provides the distinctive beer bitterness and sterilizes the wort (which is why it was initially used — old English beer recipes, dating back to 800 A.D., list yarrow leaves instead of hops, and they work very well).

The home beer maker uses sugar to avoid the complicated malting process followed by breweries. However, malt powders and whole-grain barley malts are available at wine and beer supply stores. They tend to be expensive but do produce a richer, mellower beer than that made with malt and sugar.

11. The citric acid or lemon juice added to the wort breaks down the sucrose in the sugar (which is not fermentable) into glucose and fructose, both of which are fermentable. The ascorbic acid (vitamin C) added during bottling prevents oxidation, which happens when beer or wine comes into contact with air. The gelatin fining makes a colloidal solution which captures malt particles and dead yeast cells and carries them to the bottom of the carboy. Many breweries clarify or "polish" their beer by floating varnished hazel or beechwood chips in the wort which attract sediment and yeast cells. This is what Budweiser means by "beechwood aged."

Lord Love the Elderberry

Probably no fruit variety in California and the Pacific Northwest is as ignored as the prolific elderberry. Almost everyone agrees that the elderberry is a handsome ornamental, with its long, trailing, cream-colored blossoms and bright purple fruit. But ah, the versatility of the elderberry! Elderberry jelly is an epicurean delight, and, dried or ripe, the berries make a superb sweet dessert wine, a memorable port, or a saucy dry red table wine (see page 222). But the least-known delight of the elderberry plant is certainly the airy, sunny crispness of Elderberry Fritters.

Elderberry Fritters

2 dozen clusters of elderberry blossoms
1 cup flour
1 cup beer (or ice water)
½ teaspoon salt
½ teaspoon sugar
1 egg
2 tablespoons salad oil

Set elderberry blossoms aside. Beat other ingredients with wire whisk *only* until well blended. Keep batter as cold as possible, setting bowl in ice cubes if necessary. Dip elderberry blossoms in batter and drain off excess. Cook in hot oil until lightly browned. All *squash* blossoms — especially zucchini — are light, crisp and delicious cooked this way.

FALL

Paul's Pumpkin

We buried Paul's pumpkin today.
Snaggle-tooth fat yellow veteran
of Halloween wars . . .
of bumps in the night
necessary witches
shivering four-year-old goblins
asking trick and hoping treat.

Paul, first-born laughing sun
running through Pacific-blue California summer—
Tall Paul, three feet long
leaping pumpkins in orange haze of
Half Moon Bay pumpkin field.

(Under summer sun
Tall Paul grew a foot
and a 30-foot pumpkin vine
the year he brought home
packet of Big Max pumpkin seeds.)

Paul's pumpkin, we laughed,
stroking the cool orange rotundity
strange in the front yard.

Tall Serious Paul did not laugh—
dug and pruned
watered and waited
for Bigger Max
than all Half Moon Bay.

"You have to cut the vine,"
a grownup said
when Tall Paul couldn't reach
around Fat Orange Max,
"Cut it and let it cure."

Then Paul carved orange blaze
of Halloween glory—
Fiercely Fat Max
a friendly enough horror.

But wet November skies
stole Orange Max away.
left gray-green wrinkled pumpkin.

"He'll make fertilizer,"
said Serious Paul
hacking pale-orange Max to bits
with ceremonial shovel.

Garden Paul, garden-wise:
sprouting, cutting the vine to cure,
plowing back for next year.

Earth Tones

Big with increase, the fertile California earth, turning from the sun, has passed the autumnal equinox. I move among the late tomato vines and butterbean plants in the garden, which are bravely producing still, but nearly spent. The tomatoes and bean pods are smaller now, as the evening of the seasons passes into night. I see all around subtle November hints of winter ("The poetry of the earth is never dead," wrote John Keats): the bold, fat and green grasshoppers; the peeper frogs and katydids singing louder now, a defiant last chorus against the numbing winter rains; leaves, not crisped by frost but by the searing dry summer of the Napa Valley, windblown and restless in the streets.

These signs of fall bring back autumnal images still bright from childhood. For me it is hand-husking field corn and tossing the picked ears with a loud bang against the sideboard of the horse-drawn wagon. Or gathering plump white hickory nuts one day while irritated squirrels rained nuts down on us (with impish accuracy) from a hickory tree that is still golden in memory. And who doesn't remember that pile of leaves too good not to dive into, and the laughter of friends as we emerged breathless from the musty interior trying to shake bits of leaves out of our clothes. With memories so thick and ripe as these, autumn seems the natural time for taking measure of growth — in ourselves as well as in the land.

In the springtime of his life, the young William Shakespeare wrote the exuberant comedies *A Midsummer Night's Dream* and *The Taming of the Shrew*. Later plays such as *King Lear* and *The Tempest* are suffused with an autumnal tone — a harvest of human ambition, treachery, love, deceit and longing. "Men must endure their going hence," he wrote in *King Lear,* "even as their coming hither: Ripeness is all."

"Ripeness is all," autumn tells us, with its looming, orange Harvest Moon and its timeless blue suspension of haze on the distant hills. In the clarity of a fall day, even time seems to ripen, to grow full and plump and round.

One russet-and-gold late October afternoon this past autumn I was splitting clear-grained white oak chunks for the fireplace. In the back yard the late fall sun, slanting through the scarlet, orange and yellow leaves of maple and sycamore, turned the air a palpable buttery yellow. The smell of frying chicken drifted from the house — country fried chicken, soaked in milk, then floured and fried slowly in lard and butter. Along with it would be peppery chicken gravy and baking powder biscuits for supper.

The double-bitted axe swung easily. The oak chunks sliced apart in sharp-edged columns of clean, tan-and-cream wood. Woodsmoke from the house drifted low to the ground in whorls of blue. Only when the sun slipped behind the Mayacamas Mountains to the west did the chill drive me to the warm bustle of the house, and even then, in the still twilight, that fall day seemed suspended, timeless, as if it might be going to go on forever.

Country Fried Chicken

Freshly ground pepper, lots of it, and milk are the secrets to the rich, full taste of country fried chicken. The lard-butter mixture and slow frying ensure a crackling crispness. Any cooking oil, of course, may be substituted, but the final product, while excellent, won't taste the same.

1 frying chicken, cut into serving pieces
Milk
Tabasco sauce
 1 tablespoon or more freshly ground black pepper
¼ pound lard
¼ pound butter or magarine
All-purpose flour
Salt to taste

Cover the chicken with milk in a mixing bowl, adding a few drops of Tabasco or Louisiana hot sauce and about half a teaspoon of black pepper. Let stand for an hour or longer or, better yet, refrigerate overnight.

Begin melting the lard and butter in a large, heavy skillet. Drain the milk from the chicken. In a large bowl, place enough flour to coat the chicken. Add salt to taste and the remaining black pepper. Dredge chicken pieces in flour. Let stand a few minutes to "set" the flour coating. As the lard and butter melt, add the chicken, skin side down. Cook chicken on high heat until it is crispy brown on the skin side, then turn the pieces gently with tongs. Reduce heat to moderately low and finish cooking until crispy brown on the other side. Cook slowly at least 20 minutes. Drain well on paper towels.

Fried Rabbit and Squirrel

Both domesticated and wild rabbit and squirrel are delicious when country fried exactly like the chicken in the recipe above. Wild rabbit and squirrel improve in flavor when cut into serving pieces and soaked overnight in a salt-water solution (2 tablespoons salt per quart of water). Also, older or mature cottontail rabbit or squirrel may be tenderized by parboiling for 15 minutes and letting cook before preparing for frying.

GATHERING:
A Natural Harvest
from Land and Sea

Everything that lives is holy . . . and most of it, with proper respect, can be gathered and eaten.

The Indians of California and the Pacific Northwest found food nearly everywhere they turned. Both game and seafood were extravagantly available in the coastal areas. Berries and mushrooms led the list of delicious wild plant foods, but the diversity of other natural edible foods provided a varied diet. The Indians ate elderberry flowers deep-fried in bear grease (see Elderberry Fritters, page 155) and made a cooling summer drink from the ripe berries. Boiled dock stems ("wild rhubarb"), steamed new shoots of cattail, camas and arrowhead (wapato) and skunk cabbage root frequently accompanied fish and game in tribal meals.

Today as in Indian times, imaginative cooks and food gatherers can create salads and vegetable dishes from cow parsnip, pepper grass, nettles, dock (sorrel), fireweed, horsetail, sweet coltsfoot, milkweed, ferns and shoots and stalks of salmonberry.

Some of my most memorable meals have been improvisations of what we had on hand and what we could find nearby. Summers ago, for example, my wife and I got ourselves semi-lost while hiking out of the primitive Hell's Canyon hogback ridge country on the eastern border of Oregon. Down to our last bite of food in the midmorning of our third day on the trail, I shot a wood grouse with the .22 pistol. The knapsack contained only a can of chili and a dozen crackers. We cleaned the grouse and parboiled it in a kettle over the campfire for a bit, then simmered it in the chili. Grouse chili, crackers, and draughts of nearby icy spring water remain vivid in memory as a gastronomical adventure.

Nutting Time

For children, nutting, even in a fence-row along a busy roadside (public domain, by the way, free to the thoughtful scavenger), is an exciting treasure hunt. In California and the Pacific Northwest, many tons of native black walnuts, escaped English walnuts and hazelnuts go unharvested each year. We gather a winter's supply of all these nuts by looking along two-lane blacktop roads and by asking for gathering permission from landowners who obviously are leaving their nuts unharvested. Our English walnut supply comes from two towering, veteran trees on land surrounding the neighborhood Baptist church. One year I noticed elderly church members gathering the first ripe fall of nuts and leaving the rest. I asked about the remaining nuts and was kindly invited to become a gleaner — to the amount of a bushel of English walnuts each year.

Our native black walnuts have smaller kernels than those of the Midwest, but there is nothing richer or more flavorful in all nutdom. Many persons are put off by the soggy, tight, permanently staining outer hull of black walnuts. There are three basic methods of removing the hulls. Personally, I favor my father's. (Before his health failed, he yearly gathered, cured, cracked and picked out quarts of Arkansas black walnuts to send his children each

Christmas for fudge making.) He simply wore stout shoes
and kicked at the nuts, rolling them underfoot and neatly
separating nut from hull. The hulls may also be knocked off
if you wear stout leather gloves. But I also admire the old
country way of hulling: dump the nuts in your driveway
(gravel is preferable for obvious reason) and, after you have
driven over them for a week, pick up the hulled meats.

Nut Breads

The possibilities of using the nuts we gather are
endless, especially with Christmas coming and the need for
candies, cookies and cakes. But I tend to favor nut breads, in
many ways the ideal dessert. They are easier to make than
light bread or cakes, they contain less sugar and more
wholesome ingredients than most candy or cakes, and they
admit to an infinite variety of flavors.

The first recipe given here is also a flavorful way of
using that inevitable over-supply of zucchini that comes to
curse the industrious gardener. When the neighbors smile
wanly at your third consecutive offer of free zucchini in two
weeks, consider freezing it for winter nut bread. A delicious
rhubarb nut bread can be made from the same recipe. In nut
bread, rhubarb, a turn-off to many people when prepared
other ways, develops a smooth, mellow tang everyone can
fully appreciate.

Zucchini Nut Bread

1½ cups brown sugar (packed)
⅔ cup Crisco
1 egg
1 cup buttermilk
1 teaspoon salt
1 teaspoon soda
1 teaspoon vanilla
2½ cups sifted flour
1½ cups diced, cooked zucchini
½ cup chopped nuts

Mix in order given, alternating dry ingredients and buttermilk. Mix well. Put in 2 greased bread pans or 5 small loaf pans. Bake at 350° for 1 hour for large pans, 35 minutes for small pans. For rhubarb nut bread, substitute 1½ cups diced, raw rhubarb for the zucchini.

Strawberry Nut Bread

Here is a way to combine the strawberry jam you made last July with the nuts you gathered in October.

　1 cup butter or margarine
1½ cup sugar
　1 teaspoon vanilla
　¼ teaspoon lemon extract
　4 eggs
　3 cups flour
　¾ teaspoon cream of tartar
　½ teaspoon soda
　1 teaspoon salt
　1 cup strawberry jam
　¼ cup sour cream or buttermilk
　½ cup chopped nuts

Cream butter, sugar, vanilla and lemon extract. Add eggs one at a time. Add dry ingredients alternately with strawberry jam and sour cream or buttermilk. Add chopped nuts. Put into two well-greased bread pans and bake at 350° for 50 to 60 minutes.

Banana Nut Bread

There are as many varieties of banana nut breads as there are varieties of bananas and nuts, but this one, from Helen Dale, my mother-in-law, is the true crispy-outside, moist-inside, lightly sweet treasure.

2 cups sifted flour
2 teaspoons baking powder
½ teaspoon soda
¾ teaspoon salt
½ cup sugar
1 cup chopped nuts
¼ cup vegetable oil
1 cup mashed, dead-ripe bananas (they can't be *too* black!), about 3 bananas
1 teaspoon lemon juice

Sift together dry ingredients. Add ¾ cup of the nuts. Combine the remaining ingredients and add to dry ingredients. Stir only until the flour is moistened. Pour into 2 greased bread pans. Sprinkle the remaining nuts over the top. Bake at 350° for 1 hour. If desired, pour a mixture of cinnamon, butter and sugar over the loaf when you remove from oven.

Applesauce

Fall apple-gathering is a family foraging activity still available in Northern California and the Pacific Northwest. The pink apple-blossom promise that was spring is now the warm red passion of crisp and juicy Ben Davis, Stayman Winesap, Northern Spy and Delicious apples, plumped and colored by the cool autumn nights. Because apples grow so plentifully in this region, many growers allow families to pick their own for a minimal cost. For the past few years our family has picked the winter supply of putting-up apples for from 5¢ to 10¢ a pound. Years ago, we regularly gathered apples from abandoned orchards along lonely upland roads in Washington's Okanogan Valley north and west of Spokane. The room-filling smell of freshly gathered apples stored in pantry, closet or basement brings autumn directly to the senses.

Cinnamon Applesauce

I never knew a child who didn't like applesauce. In our family a newly opened quart jar barely lasts two meals. If you have time to do only one thing with apples, consider applesauce. Not only is it one of the simplest forms of preserving, it is also a form of putting by that delights children — especially if they help make the cinnamon applesauce described here:

Wash, quarter and core cooking apples. In a large kettle, add water barely to cover and cook until nearly soft. For 5 pounds of apples, add ½ cup sugar, 2 teaspoons lemon juice and ¼ cup small, round red-hot cinnamon candies (may be varied to suit individual taste). Cook a little bit longer, then press through a strainer or run through food mill, discarding skin. To store, pack at once, as hot as possible, into hot, scalded jars. Process in pressure canner at 5 pounds pressure for 5 minutes. Children, of course, delight in adding cinnamon red-hots to applesauce, which not only give it the cinnamon flavor but impart a delicate pink blush to the sauce.

Gifts from the Sea

Ah, the sweet abundance of seafood along the Pacific coast. There are not only the deep-sea varieties, which most of us can buy fresh at markets, but there is an astounding diversity of life to be gathered and enjoyed along the coasts and in the bays of California, Oregon and Washington.

My most unforgettable seafood experience was a week spent in a rented wooden cabin on Dabob Bay near the small town of Quilcene on the Olympic Peninsula in Washington. The cabin included access to an incredibly seafood-rich strip of beach along the shallow, sandy bay that opens off the Hood Canal. When the tide was out, we could turn up a half-bucketful of butter and razor clams with a single deep pitch of a shovel. A government oyster hatchery nearby apparently enhanced the oyster population, for every low tide exposed clumps of succulent Olympia oysters, some clumps bound together in a mass of two dozen oysters. Standing knee-deep in the bay, we opened the oysters on the spot, devouring them raw with a natural seasoning of seawater remaining in the shells. Dungeness crabs were everywhere in the shallow bay. By wading with a dip net we could collect a dozen in a half-hour. Rowing to 15-foot depths, we caught tender, two-to-three-pound flounder at will.

During the week's stay we bought only bread, milk and butter at the store. We feasted on raw clams and oysters, fried clams, stuffed clams, steamed clams, fried oysters, clam chowder, oyster stew; stuffed, sautéed and poached flounder; cracked crab, deviled crab and a continuously operating pot of bouillabaisse.

To be sure, that kind of plenty is not available everywhere. And population pressures have all but eliminated some of the choice foraging for once-abundant Pismo clams, oysters, grunion and abalone. However, the intertidal waters of the West Coast still teem with a loot of good eating: clams, crabs, marine snails, periwinkles, mussels, scallops and a variety of rockfish. It's not to be passed up.

Clams

Frank Marshall is a tall, husky man who can build most anything with his hands. He now farms a half-acre homestead in Santa Rosa and works as a rigger at Mare Island Naval Shipyard in Vallejo, but he grew up in a logging and farming family on the lush banks of the St. Joe River in northern Idaho. Hunting in the woods with his older brothers, digging potatoes and drying fruit with his father, he early inherited a country self-sufficiency.

Frank slaughters, butchers and freezes his own beef. He locates free firewood in the Northern California hills and valleys, frequently snaking logs down steep hillsides with his sturdy, rebuilt pickup truck. A restless man indoors, his dark brown eyes are calm and assured when he is out in the weather hunting, digging an asparagus bed or building a new hen-house.

What Frank Marshall likes to do best, however, is dig furiously for the huge Pacific horse clam, or gaper. To do that, he twice-yearly joins the Great Clam Race in Tomales Bay, just north of San Francisco.

The horse clam is prized as seafood in some areas of the West Coast and scorned in others. Second in size only to the massive, legendary geoduck of Washington, the horse clam may be the ugliest edible seafood to be found anywhere in the world. It has a muddy-looking, dark brown two-foot-long syphon tipped at the end with two horny valves. It reaches a size of eight inches across the shell and can weigh up to four pounds. Like the geoduck, the horse clam has a body too big for its shell; great pouches of clam flesh protrude from all sides of the splotchy, brown-and-gray shell. But that flesh is pure, white, succulent clam meat that is delicious eaten every way but raw.

The horse clam is prolific; scattered up and down the Pacific coast from Alaska to San Diego are huge beds of these bivalves, generally congregating in sandy mudflats exposed at the lowest of minus tides.

Tomales Bay, located about forty miles north of San Francisco, is especially rich in oyster beds (now mostly commercial) and tidal flats inhabited by horse clams. It is a long narrow body of water running parallel to the ocean, protected from the west by the rugged ridges and headlands of Point Reyes. At the head of the bay is the resort community of Dillon Beach, and this is where Frank Marshall joins hundreds of other clam diggers at each daylight minus tide for the Great Clam Race.

On the days of minus tides, hordes of diggers set up camp in a private park near the marina. As the tide reaches its ebb, it exposes vast mud and sand flats rich in clams. A large crowd, armed with rakes, shovels, homemade circular-shovel clam diggers and dressed in everything from wet suits to hip-waders, gathers at the water's edge just below the Dillon Beach Marina, awaiting the $1 barge ride provided by the marina to the flats, located about a quarter-mile offshore. Meanwhile, boats launched at the marina race at top speed towards the clamflats as a heady, festive excitement grips the crowd, everyone anxious to be first to reach choice digging spots.

Frank Marshall shakes his head and laughs at the frequently bizarre antics of some of the clam hunters.

"One mornin' I was waiting for the barge with my wife, Sandy, and we see this dude splashing along the shore tryin' to hitch-hike from the boats racing to the beds. He was dressed in rubber skin suit, snorkel face mask and was floppin' along in big swim flippers. He was actually mad, put out, that none of the boats would stop for him, an' he starts yellin' at the 'capitalist pigs' in the boats. Nobody ever did pick him up, and he had to swim out to the banks. I don't know if he had to swim back with his rake and tow sack full of clams or not."

Digging for horse clams is simple but hard work. The clams do not move, but depend on their depth (three to four feet) for protection. However, the industrious digger can easily get his day's limit of ten (a very large supply of clams, considering their meatiness). First locate the large, depressed holes where the long syphon emerges. Digging quickly down about three feet to water-bearing sand, find the syphon hole and slip your hand along the large syphon and beneath the clam, gently pulling it up through the loose sand. Once the hole is begun, it can be enlarged and, in productive beds, surrounding clams easily located.

The rough, grotesque syphon, the gray-and-brown splotched shell and the definite sandiness of the horse clam probably prevent many seafood fanciers from enjoying this delicacy. Frank Marshall "sweetens" his clams by taking them home in covered buckets of seawater. He then adds a double-handful of cornmeal to the water two days in a row, and the clams expel their sand and replace it with cornmeal. The ugly, meaty siphon becomes choice white clam meat when boiled a few minutes and easily stripped of its skin. The siphon can be slit open, cut into four-inch pieces, pounded well and sautéed in flour or cornmeal like abalone; while it doesn't taste just like abalone, it is superb clam.

When he steams his clams, Frank Marshall carefully pours off the rich clam juice or nectar, leaving behind any sand or meal refuse. He carefully washes the meat in the juice, then runs it through a food grinder. Clam meat can be frozen for future clam chowder or clam patties.

Clam Patties

1 cup ground horse clam meat
1 egg
½ cup bread crumbs or fine cracker meal

Moisten hands and mix together egg, bread crumbs and clam meat, then shape into hamburger-size patties. Fry in a small amount of oil over medium heat.

Overlooked Clams   The availability of clams on the Pacific Coast increases the farther north we go — chiefly because of the pocked, ragged nature of the coastline from Humboldt Bay in California north to island-studded Puget Sound and the fjord-laced coast of British Columbia. The once-abundant butter clam, the prize of Washington beaches, sounds and inlets, however, is diminishing in numbers due to population pressures. Spring minus tides are the best times to dig these small, plump delicacies that are delicious raw, steamed, fried or in chowder. The large, meaty western razor clam, also highly prized, must now be sought in the farthest low-tide reaches of open, sandy beach. The elusive razor moves swiftly through packed sand, both vertically and horizontally, so considerable art and dexterity are needed to extract this disappearing creature. The razor clam digger pats the surface of the sand with his spade if he suspects one is present. If it is, a small watery pit will appear — the sign of a disappearing razor clam. At this point, the digger has one swift chance to quickly thrust the shovel under the clam, cutting off escape, and throw it to the surface. Once on the surface, the clam must be put in a bag or bucket, or it will slip rapidly back into the sand.

Crowbar Clams   The serious and experienced clam digger of the West Coast often heads for the beach armed with a crowbar or rockbar and pick in addition to a clam shovel and rake. Some of the tastiest and most plentiful clams along the lower Oregon and Northern California coast are permanently embedded — and hidden — in burrows in stiff clay and soft rock along tide-swept beaches and reefs.

I learned the secret of locating and digging these boring clams (the western rough piddock and cancellatus) from Portuguese farming and fishing families descended from the original settlers of Half Moon Bay. At low tides, the diggers start chipping away at the stiff clay deposits that shelve out into the surf. The bluish-to-buff-colored deposits are formed in layers that frequently chip off in large slabs, revealing the burrows dug by energetic boring clams. With luck, a slab of removed clay will expose as many as two dozen clams, some four to five inches across the shell.

Boring clams are satisfyingly meaty. Somewhat like the horse clam, the borer has a body too large for its shell, which gapes open at both ends. One end of the shell has rough, rasplike teeth with which the borer digs, continuously enlargening and cleaning out its burrow.

Because they do not long survive out of their burrows, and because of their rough, gaping appearance, boring clams are not found in markets on the West Coast. The meat is excellent, however, and they are easy to clean. Small borers are succulent when steamed and dipped in melted butter. The larger ones are best when put through the meat grinder and prepared as Clam Patties (page 181), stuffed clams or clam chowder. The large syphon, which may be an inch in diameter and a foot long when extended, is excellent clam meat.

Mussels

One of the blind sides in American taste is mussels, which are grown for consumption in the coastal waters of France and highly prized as seafood. Yet in years of gathering mussels along the California coast, I have rarely come across anyone else gathering mussels for anything but fishbait.

My wife Cindy-Irene loves mussels but had never gathered them until a few years ago when we took a foraging outing near San Francisco. The destination was just south of Half Moon Bay, where my daughter lives on a ranch with a half mile of ocean frontage. Overlooked by steep clay bluffs, a large rock just offshore from a small cove creates a shallow, sandy, protected lagoon at low tide, perfect for children to splash and swim in safely. (For a fee of $1 per car, the public is permitted access.) It was on that offshore rock that we were gathering.

Cindy-Irene disappeared from view while I was puttering about among the small mussels and hermit crabs in crevices along the top of the rock. Then, through the roar of the waves, I heard her excited yell. She had climbed twenty feet down the vertical seaward face of the rock. There, in her blue polka-dot bikini, the implacable surf sending gouts of green water over her feet and legs, she was clinging to the rock with one hand and excitedly waving a huge six-inch mussel with the other.

"I found the big ones!" she shouted over the roar, "Send down the bucket!" Not really wanting to watch, I lowered the bucket, which she filled in a few minutes.

On our way back to the highway we purchased four massive artichokes from a field-side stand near the beach. We stopped later to buy a crusty loaf of Sonoma French bread and a bottle of Wente Brothers Johannisberg Riesling.

Once home we debearded the mussels and scrubbed the shells with a plastic mesh scrubber. Cindy-Irene put the artichokes on to steam and then launched into preparing the fabled Mussels Mariniére.

The judicious Craig Claiborne, food editor of the *New York Times,* is given to New England understatement in most of his recommendations. But he prefaces the Mussles Mariniére recipe in the *New York Times Cookbook* by stating, correctly, that "this is one of the most glorious dishes ever created."

Mussels Mariniére

6 tablespoons butter
1 clove garlic, chopped
3 tablespoons chopped shallot
or onion
2 small leeks, chopped
1 small bay leaf
3 dozen fresh mussels,
scrubbed well and debearded**

¾ cup dry white wine
4 teaspoons flour
½ cup cream
2 egg yolks
Chopped parsley
Salt and freshly ground
black pepper to taste

In a deep kettle or saucepan, heat 3 tablespoons of the butter, add the garlic and shallot and cook over low heat 1 minute. Add leeks and bay leaf and cook 2 minutes longer.

Add mussels, sprinkle with salt and pepper and pour the wine over the top. Cover and simmer gently until the mussel shells open, about 10 minutes. Remove the mussels, discard the top shell but leave the mussel in the bottom shell. Arrange in soup dishes.

Strain the liquid in the saucepan and bring to a boil. Thicken slightly with *beurre manié*, made by creaming the remaining butter with the flour. Remove saucepan from heat and add the cream mixed with the egg yolks.

Heat the sauce, without letting it boil, and pour over the mussels. Sprinkle with finely chopped parsley and serve immediately.

"Mussels Marinére" from *The New York Times Cookbook* by Craig Claiborne Copyright ©1961 by Craig Claiborne, Reprinted by permission of Harper & Row, Publishers, Inc.

**Simply clip the "beards" with scissors.

Mussel Fritters

Children who are suspicious of any seafoods besides deep-fried shrimp tend to love this dish. Your friends will eat all you can gather if the mussels are fried this way.

3 to 4 dozen mussels
1 egg
2 tablespoons water
1 cup fine cracker or bread crumbs
Salt and pepper to taste

Steam the mussels in a deep kettle with ½ cup water until they open wide. Remove meats to a separate bowl and discard shells. Beat egg slightly with the water and pour over mussels. Stir until mussel meat is evenly coated. Drain the coated mussels briefly in a sieve or colander. Put the bread or cracker crumbs and salt and pepper in a brown paper bag. Pour in the mussels and shake gently until mussels are coated with the crumbs and separate. Fry in oil on medium heat until golden brown, about 3 minutes. Drain on paper towels and serve hot, garnished with chopped parsley and lemon wedges.

Steamed Mussels in White Wine

Elegant, yet one of the easiest seafood dishes of all to prepare. Place 3 to 4 dozen mussels in a deep kettle, add ½ cup white wine, cover, and steam for 20 minutes. Discard any mussels that do not open. Remove the top shells and arrange in soup dishes. Strain the broth, reheat and pour over the mussels-on-the-halfshell. Dip crusty French bread in the broth while enjoying the purple and pale-orange mussels. Seafood-loving French families polish off this many mussels before moving on to the main dinner course.

Gourmet Dining at the Tide Table

For several years my family and I lived in an ocean-front house perched on a bluff over extensive tide pools in Moss Beach, a tiny community about fifteen miles south of San Francisco. Needless to say, we ate regularly from the sea. In fact, the whole family became so used to foraging on the beach at low tides for clams and mussels, and fishing off the outer rock reef for green, rock, and ling cod, surf perch, and cabazone, that the question, "What's on the tide table tonight?" was asked almost daily.

It was also during those years that we became acquainted — thanks to the Filipino fishermen in the area — with some unexpected seafood delicacies that are usually ignored by uninitiated clam diggers and abalone hunters: sea urchin and whelks and marine snails. The red-brown and dark purple giant urchin abounds in rock reefs from Alaska to Mexico, and is, indeed, considered something of a pest because of its habit of burrowing into and devouring coral and rock ledges. In late autumn and winter the giant urchin is found with huge, swelling roe sacks, bright orange in color, inside the bottom, or open, end of the test, or thin shell. This roe, eaten raw, is delicious, with a superbly delicate oyster flavor. It is too delicate to cook. Simply turn the urchin over, open side up, and crack midway around the test with a rock or hammer. Discard the viscera with the top (closed) half and scoop out the bright orange roe from the five-pointed egg sac found against the upper part of the test.

If the urchins can be eaten within a few hours, they may be taken home and the roe spread on slices of crusty French bread. Many Italian fishing families in San Francisco have been enjoying this delicacy for generations.

Salt-Water Escargot

All of the marine snails and whelks found along the California, Oregon and Washington coast are edible. The large, tough foot of the big moon shell snail can be removed from the cracked shell, cleaned of viscera, sliced into half-inch steaks, tenderized, pounded and cooked like sautéed abalone. Smaller marine snails and the large dog whelks should be boiled in sea or salt water for 15 to 20 minutes and removed from the shell with a nutpick. These bite-sized bits may then be lightly sautéed in butter and garlic and served on toast, accompanied by a well-chilled white wine.

Furthermore, the boiled meat of moon shells and whelks may be put through a meat grinder and used as a base for a flavorful chowder prepared the same way as clam chowder.

Be bold. It's all out there for the eating.

West Coast Clambake!

    With the makings so close at hand, you won't find a better excuse for an old-fashioned gathering of friends and family than a clambake. The process is simple, but there is enough to do to give everyone the satisfaction of having taken part. Put that together with the gustatory treat — freshly cooked clams and mussels right out of the shell; fish fillets, juicy and steaming in their wrappers — and you have a day that no one will soon forget.

    Our foraging expeditions during low tide around Half Moon Bay used to supply enough seafood —literally a car trunk full — to feed two dozen people. While some of us gathered mussels and boring clams, others picked up hermit crabs for bait and bottom-fished off the outer reefs, which are exposed at low tide. When the tide turns, rockfish feed frenziedly — fat, bluish surf perch, rock cod, green cod and an occasional voracious ling cod, a highly prized eating fish which also smokes very well. (If foraging in your area is inadequate, it can be supplemented with seafood purchased fresh from a market. You can distribute the expense by inviting your guests to purchase and bring whatever seafood they fancy.)

    We also gather wet seaweed. Laid over the bed of coals, this provides a tangy steam to do the cooking. Wet cornshucks may also be used, alone or in combination with seaweed. During sweet corn season, the ideal clambake time, green cornshucks may be used for wrapping the fish fillets as well.

The other basic ingredients for a clambake are whole potatoes and sweet corn, either from your own garden or purchased from a supplier of fresh vegetables.

The process is as follows:
At the beach or in your back yard, dig a trench 2 feet deep, 2 feet wide and 6 to 8 feet long. Line with large stones. Build a log fire in the whole trench and let burn for at least two hours, adding logs as necessary. When the fire is down to mostly coals, remove the unburnt logs and rake coals out evenly. Cover the coals with 4 to 6 inches of wet seaweed, well-soaked cornshucks or green cornshucks, or a mixture of these. Lay whole, scrubbed potatoes on this. Cover with a thin layer of seaweed or shucks. Then lay in ears of fresh sweet corn from which the outer shucks have been removed. Distribute among these the clams and fish fillets. (Prepare fillets by wrapping them, along with slivers of onion, dots of butter and chopped parsley, in foil or in green cornshucks.) The clams and fish will be easier to locate after cooking if put in berry boxes or shallow wire baskets (serious East Coast clambakers fashion their own shallow wire baskets to hold the seafood). In addition to the clams, mussels and fish fillets, scallops and crabs also cook perfectly this way.

When the corn and seafood are distributed in the pit, cover with another 4-inch layer of seaweed and/or cornshucks; then cover all this with an old tarp, sheet of tin roofing or piece of plywood and seal around the edges with stones or dirt to retain the heat and steam. Cook for one hour. Since the heat will vary from fire to fire, it is wise to uncover a corner to test the food for doneness before uncovering the whole pit, raking back the seaweed and shucks and removing the food.

Puget Sound Clambakes and Halibut Cheeks

I once spent two summers working on a commercial salmon boat that operated out of the tiny village of Neah Bay on the western tip of the Olympic Peninsula — the westernmost town in the United States. Many Hoh, Makah and Quinault Indians still fish for halibut and salmon from their traditional forty-foot dugout canoes hollowed from western red cedar logs — the younger fishermen madly whizzing their canoes, powered by 75-horsepower Evinrude motors, about the cannery dock pilings.

Although we tend to think of the clambake as an invention of the Indians and settlers of New England, it also dates back to the origins of Indian cookery in the Pacific Northwest. The Hoh and Quinault Indians, on festive occasions, follow the traditional method of digging a wide pit on the beach, lining it with smooth stones and building a large fire. When it dies down, they place wet leaves or seaweed on the hot stones and add butter, mud, geoduck and razor clams, mussels, crab and halibut and salmon fillets wrapped in leaves. They place a mat or layer of seaweed over the seafood, first pouring hot water over it all, leaving it to steam for about an hour.

While trolling for salmon in the deep, icy waters off Puget Sound, we frequently caught huge "whale" halibut (to commercial fishermen, "whale" halibut are those weighing over forty pounds. Halibut as large as four hundred pounds are not uncommon in the waters from Puget Sound north to Alaska). I learned from grizzled Matt McClannahan, a third-generation salmon fisherman who operated his troller *Suzy-Q* the year around out of Neah Bay and also Prince Rupert, British Columbia, that one of the greatest delicacies to come aboard the boat was halibut cheeks. This is a firm, exceptionally tender fillet (as large as a half-pound each on large halibut) that can be scooped out of each cheek on the wide, flat head of the fish. Matt and most of the halibut and salmon fishermen I knew saved the prized cheeks for themselves. Many of the fishermen ate the halibut cheeks raw, and I assumed that this was carefully cultivated *macho,* a part of the fishing mystique. Then I tasted them. Drizzled with lemon and freshly ground pepper, raw halibut cheeks are a tender delicacy unlike anything else in seafood — the flesh seems to melt in your mouth.

Because many fishermen save the cheeks for themselves and because "whale" halibut are now less common in their southern range around Puget Sound, a century-old Seattle food tradition is slowly disappearing: creamed halibut cheeks served on toast, a Sunday brunch favorite of old Seattle. The cheeks, then available at most fresh fish markets, were generally purchased on Saturday. For Sunday brunch they were gently poached for a few minutes and then warmed in a medium white sauce (the recipes variously incorporating a touch of dill, rosemary or fennel) and served over toast. Even today, many native Seattleites become dreamily nostalgic at the mention of creamed halibut cheeks. Today, however, hotels, specialty restaurants and the fishermen themselves consume most of the available supply.

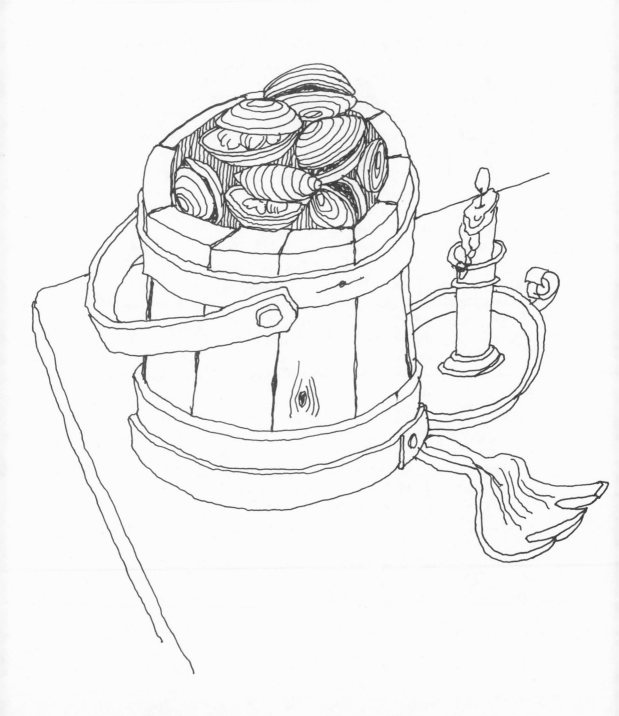

Washpot Clambake

While living in the small college town of Cheney, about twenty miles south of Spokane, Washington, I spent many satisfying weekends foraging outdoors and fishing with Dick Bresgal. Dick was a tall, rangy Washington native, a superb trout fisherman, an accomplished poet and a reluctant railroad brakeman.

Dick Bresgal showed me the favorite haunts of rainbow and brook trout in the Spokane River all the way from the Idaho border, through downtown Spokane, to its confluence with the Columbia River just south of the Okanogan Valley. He also organized weekend trips to the Washington coast, to Bellingham, his boyhood home, where he used to rent a friend's 18-foot boat and take us on an hour's trip from Bellingham Bay to nearby isolated islands in the San Juans. There, during low tide, we dug clams, netted Dungeness crabs and bottom-fished for flounder and rockfish.

We dressed out the flounder and packed them in ice chests as soon as they were caught. We stored our limits of razor, butter and littleneck clams in five-gallon cans filled with seawater.* The crabs we stowed in a large washtub packed to the brim with seaweed.

Returning home with our catch, plus seawater and seaweed, we gathered to help Dick Bresgal prepare his locally famous Washpot Clambake. Dick used a large copper washpot for his stove-top clambakes, but a large enamel pot, such as a canner, will do quite well:

---

*Like the Japanese, or Pacific, oyster, the Eastern littleneck clam has found a second home in the coastal waters of the Pacific Northwest; both have "gone native" and now flourish there.

1 washpot or large enamel pot
Seaweed (washed, since clam liquor will be served)
1 quart seawater (or fresh water)
Crabs
Clams
Fish fillets wrapped in foil or green corn shucks (see West
    Coast Clambake, page 190)
Scrubbed potatoes
Sweet corn, outer husks removed

Fill the bottom of the washpot or enamel pot with about 4 inches of seaweed. Add the water and turn heat to high. Add potatoes and another layer of seaweed and cover. Allow to boil 15 minutes, then add the fish fillets and another layer of seaweed and cover. Fifteen minutes later add the crabs and more seaweed and cover. After 10 and 20 minutes, respectively, add the corn and clams; keep covered. Steam until the clams open. Serve with melted butter and crusty bread. Serve the kettle liquor in heated bowls as a dip.

From Flounder to Dab

From the Catalina Islands off Los Angeles to Puget Sound, more than a dozen varieties of cottom-feeding flat fish may be caught by shore, breakwater and pier fishermen. They include the petrale sole, sand dab, halibut, white flounder and lemon, or English, sole. None of these are true sole; with the exception of the halibut, they are technically dabs.

These fish are easily caught during the right seasons of the year, and the firm, lean, white and relatively boneless flesh of the dabs is perhaps the finest fresh seafood available in California and the Pacific Northwest. They are best when prepared simply: Sautéed in butter, broiled with a lemon-butter sauce, rolled in flour and lightly fried, or poached in a court bouillon, the dabs are seafood at its best.

The Indians in the Pacific Northwest have a centuries-long relationship with fish and have developed some of the best — and simplest — methods I know of cooking it. When stormy weather occasionally shut down salmon trolling out of Neah Bay, I used to spend long hours gathering fishing lore and seafood recipes from the Indian families along the coast of the Olympic Peninsula, where the traditional methods of fishing, cooking and preserving are still in use. The recipes which follow, some of them adjusted or modified by me over the years, come from those traditions and are marked by the Indians' ability to make the most of the natural good flavor of fish.

Flounder in Mussel Sauce

2 dozen mussels, scrubbed and debearded
½ cup water
8 fillets of flounder, sole or sand dab
3 eggs
1 cup flour
2 teaspoons salt
½ cup butter or margarine
½ cup minced chives
Freshly ground black pepper to taste
Chopped parlsey to garnish

Add the water to the mussels in a large kettle; cover and steam for 15 minutes. Remove mussels from the shell and chop. Reserve ½ cup of the mussel broth. Beat the eggs lightly in a shallow pan. Place flour, salt and pepper in another shallow pan. Dip the fish in the egg and then in the flour, coating evenly. Let fillets stand for 30 minutes for coating to "set" — preferably in the refrigerator. Add butter or margarine to a large skillet. Brown fillets on both sides over medium heat. In another skillet melt 2 tablespoons butter or margarine; add mussels, chives and the ½ cup of mussel broth and simmer for at least 5 minutes. Pour mussel sauce over fillets on a large, hot platter. Garnish with chopped parsley and ring with lemon wedges.

"Clambake" Halibut

This is a back yard — or kitchen — variation of the Northwest Indian clambake. The recipe here provides for cooking on the barbecue grill. If prepared in the oven, place the foil-wrapped package in a shallow pan.

2 dozen mussels or small clams
2 pounds halibut fillets
¼ cup butter or margarine
2 green onions, sliced, including tops
½ teaspoon dill or rosemary
Salt and freshly ground black pepper to taste
Minced parsley

Lay the halibut fillets in the middle of a large piece of heavy-duty foil. Dot with butter or margarine and sprinkle with onions, dill or rosemary and parsley. Salt and pepper to taste. Place mussels or clams on the fish. Fold over aluminum foil and seal the edges tightly to retain juice. Place on the barbecue grill and cook for 45 minutes covered. Remove foil, lay fish on grill to smoke and cook for 15 minutes (45 minutes in 350° oven). The clam or mussel nectar will poach the halibut to ambrosian goodness.

Salmon: The "Spirit People"

To the Hoh, Kwakiutl, Salish and Bella Coola Indian tribes of Washington and British Columbia, salmon were not just fish but a race of "spirit people" who lived in a magic village deep in the ocean. During the annual spring and summer spawning migrations in oceans and rivers, the "spirit people" willingly swarmed upriver to feed their fellow human race, the Indians. The solemn, reverent Indian ceremony of the first salmon was a recognition of this great gift. The first salmon caught was carefully laid out on the riverbank with its head upstream so that the other fish would continue to follow. The Indians spoke of the "Five Tribes" of salmon that correspond to the five species that migrate up Western rivers today.

Preparing for winter's food, the Indian men netted and speared the swarming salmon from coastal rivers while the women gathered mussels, clams, scallops and barnacles from tide pools and flats. The shellfish were alder-smoked and stored on skewers for winter; the salmon was smoked and dried for preservation. Indeed, the Indian tribal name *Kwakiutl* means 'smoke of the world'.

Thus, the beneficence of the Great Spirit brought together, in one part of the earth, the wood of the alder and the firm pink flesh of the salmon — a truly epicurean combination.

I first learned of the flavor affinity between alder smoke and fresh fish from Johnny Two-Fingers, a Nez-Perce Indian woodsman who hunted and fished the rugged Wallowa Mountains in eastern Oregon. Carrying cooking and camping gear, my wife and I were fishing our way down the headwaters of the remote, tumultuous Imnaha River in the uninhabited Snake River Canyon area of the Oregon-Idaho border. Because of its relative inaccessibility to fishermen, the swift, clear Imnaha was a superb trout stream, crowded with sixteen-inch native rainbow and brook trout. We had spent two days catching and releasing trout in every pool, using hand-tied wooly-worm wet flies. The only other people we had seen were occasional kamikaze rubber-rafters who would zip into view around a bend, spin crazily in out-of-control circles in the stretch of channel or rapids before us and disappear, tilted crazily on a large wave, at the first downriver bend.

On the third day out we had made camp on a grassy shelf above a rare gravel bar beach, the pup tent tucked under four drooping red willow trees. We were cleaning the day's catch of firm brookies for the evening meal — brook trout wrapped with bacon, spitted down the center with a green willow stick and grilled over oak coals.

I was crouched at the water's edge scaling trout when I heard a whoop and looked up to see a rubber raft shoot around the upriver bend. In it was a short, muscular Indian with shoulder-length hair. He waved his paddle overhead, then dug it into the water, propelling the raft to the beach. The rafter explained that he was fishing his way to the little town of Imnaha, about thirty miles downstream, something he did several times each summer, and asked if he could buy leader material from us, having lost his to rocks and smart trout. We gladly shared ours in exchange for his freely offered advice on the best fishing pools and riffles in the river.

Invited to share our campfire to cook his evening meal of trout, Johnny Two-Fingers eyed our preparations for spitted, grilled trout curiously.

"Whitefaces cook okay, but get mushy trout," he said, revealing a mock drugstore-Indian irony that obliquely asserted his deep Nez-Perce pride and sense of humor (to this day, Johnny Two-Fingers sends us annual "Happy Custer's Day" cards).

With his large hunting knife, Johnny cut a green willow pole four feet long and one inch in diameter. He split the pole down the center for a distance of about eighteen inches and cut six slender green willow branches into two-foot lengths, slitting each one. Then he sliced his trout down the backbone so they laid flat. He inserted three of the willow branches crossways in the split section of the pole, laid the trout across them, then gently wedged three more split branches across the top of the trout and tied the end of the split pole with one turn of green willow bark, making a wooden rack in an operation that took only about ten minutes. To the oak in our already-burning fire he added some dried alder logs and cut a few lengths of slender green alder. When the fire burned down to coals he added more green alder and cooked our trout in the rack held over the coals, three to five minutes per side. From that day on, we have cooked trout and salmon by that method whenever possible (using, however, an easily-portable folding metal rack for the fish).

Johnny Two-Fingers pointed out, and we later confirmed, that just about every Northwest Indian tribe cooked salmon and trout by his method. To this day, Indians along the Columbia River and around Puget Sound alder-smoke salmon to eat fresh or slow-smoke it for winter storage — and to sell to tourists.

Smoked Fish

Most oceanside communities in California and the Pacific Northwest have commercial smokehouses where fishermen can take their salmon, barracuda, ling cod or smelt to be smoked. But with a small amount of ingenuity, any fisherman can smoke fish right at home. A smoker may be purchased at sporting-goods stores or rigged from an old refrigerator, oil drum or metal garbage can. A hot-plate and a pan full of hickory or alder chips does the job in the last three rigs, but one can also smoke fish satisfactorily on a covered barbecue grill — or even on an open grill covered with a cardboard box.

There are two methods of smoking fish — cold smoking and hot smoking. Cold smoking is done at a comparatively lower temperature (150° to 170° F) over a longer period of time. Fish cold-smoked in a homemade smoker or smokehouse is more deeply smoked and dried and will keep indefinitely in a cool, dry place. Hot-smoked fish will keep in the refrigerator for a month or so. For both methods the basic process is the same.

Smoking Preparations   Prepare a brine of one cup noniodized salt per gallon of water. Soak fish fillets, split fish or whole small fish 45 minutes in the brine. Small fish larger than smelt should be split down along the backbone and laid out flat with belly skin intact. Hang small fish on a rack or lay them with fillets on a grill.

Smoking Methods   In the smoker, place a pound of hickory or alder chips in a pan on a hot-plate with just enough heat to make the chips smoulder and smoke. Provide a small vent at the top. To cold smoke, maintain a heat of 150° to 175° for 1½ to 2 hours. To hot smoke, maintain a heat of 250° for 45 minutes.

If the smoking is done over a barbecue grill, soak a pound of hickory chips or alder chips for an hour in water. Build a very small charcoal fire (coals an inch or two apart when raked out) and spread ignited coals across the whole grill. Place the soaked chips on the fire, put fish on the grill as far from the fire as possible and cover, leaving a small vent open.

The best fish for smoking are small to medium-size fish split along the backbone. Whenever possible, leave the skin on. Bones are no problem, since the smoked fish will separate from the bones. Many indifferent-tasting fresh fish smoke beautifully, including sturgeon, carp, suckers and mullet. Barracuda, generally despised by sport fishermen, smokes to a delicious, dark-red texture.

THE FALL GARDEN:
Turning Towards Winter

The passing of summer does not mean the end of this year's garden, or of the gardener's work. With the notable exception of slow-maturing crops such as onions and potatoes, most garden vegetables may be planted in mid-August as fall crops. Some flourish more than others in the cooler nights: English peas, lettuce, Swiss chard, cabbage, cauliflower, broccoli and bush green beans, for instance. English peas produce a smaller yield than when spring-planted, as do bush green beans, but they do quite well overall.

Since many areas of California and the Pacific Northwest are quite hot and arid in mid-August, the plantings at this time must be adapted to the conditions. Two basic rules here: Plant the seeds slightly deeper than for spring plantings, and keep the soil moist until the seedlings poke through the surface.

Besides the vegetables specifically mentioned here, you can make a rule-of-thumb decision about which garden vegetables will produce in the fall simply by calculating the maturing date of the vegetable and comparing it with the date of the first expected killing frost. Some vegetables, such as spinach (which thrives in cool weather), lettuce, Swiss chard, turnips, parsnips, kohlrabi and green bunching onions, will tolerate light frosts. Onions that winter over may be used as scallions, but they will have a stronger flavor than spring onions. Collards, turnips and parsnips actually pick up a sweeter flavor from light frosts.

Living in the mild winter coastal climate of California, I find that lettuce, cabbage, cauliflower and spinach will yield all winter long, but they must be planted by mid-August to establish a strong growth before November's cold, when the growth slows markedly. Each March I harvest about a bushel of wintered-over lettuce to make way for the early planting of Early Alaska peas.

Fall, of course, is storage time for the summer root crops — onions, carrots, potatoes, turnips and parsnips. The crucial thing in storing onions and potatoes is to let them cure — dry thoroughly — for a few days in a warm, shaded place. They should then be stored loosely in a cool, dry basement or cellar. Carrots will keep practically all winter if they are packed in boxes of dry sand. Onions may be braided in a string by their dry stems and hung; or the dry stems may be cut off and the onions hung in mesh bags to allow for good air circulation. The Burpee seed catalog offers mesh onion bags which, when hung in a corner of the kitchen, look colorfully garden-businesslike.

The firm winter squash varieties (such as Butternut, Hubbard, Turk's Turban and Acorn) will keep all winter if they are fully ripe, or "cured." Test this by pressing the rind with a thumbnail. If the rind doesn't give, the time for picking and storing has arrived. Handle carefully to avoid scarring the rind. Wipe the squash gently with a cloth containing mineral oil. Store loosely in a dark, cool place. Check the squash monthly and wipe with the mineral oil.

There remains the final task of putting the garden to bed for the winter. It is time to gather and plow in mulch that the winter rains and freezes will break down. Leaves,

grass clippings, stable manure and whatever vegetable
refuse you can scavenge can be laid on the garden. In some
coastal areas, seaweed is easily available and makes an
excellent mulch, high in valuable mineral content. If you
gather seaweed for mulch, hose it down well to get rid of
excess salt before putting it into the garden. You may also
scatter wood ashes on the soil (if you save them for this
purpose, try to keep them dry, since the rain quickly leaches
out much of the fertile material in wood ashes). Although it
isn't a necessary practice, I favor sowing a green cover crop
of winter rye or wheat to be plowed under in the spring. Not
only does this cover crop provide quickly decomposing
"green manure" for the spring garden, but it also adds fluffy
humus to the soil, an important addition to the caked, adobe
soils of much of California and the Southwest.

Making Wine

Some preserve or can their garden's bounty, but there's nothing to stop you from making wine with it. Once the basic, inexpensive equipment is assembled, home winemaking is a quite simple process. In light of the rewards, it is one of the most satisfying of all hobbies.

As a wine maker, I consider myself fortunate to live in the finest vinifera grape country in the United States, the Napa Valley; but over the years, I have made highly drinkable table and dessert wines from Midwestern Niagara and Steuben grapes, from wild Scuppernong grapes and from elderberries, blackberries, apples, pears, peaches, dandelion and beets.

Next to unflagging curiosity, patience is the mark of the successful wine maker. Wherever I have lived, I have sought out *Italiana* home wine makers who carry on the tradition of making the family's supply of wine. Their attitude is one of patient, thankful fatalism. If it is a good wine year they drink thankfully the simple, sturdy red with their meals. If it is a poor year they still enjoy a decent dinner wine. One has to be either very careless or use an entirely unsuited grape — like Thompson Seedless — to make a *bad* wine.

A partner in wine making and I once produced thirty
gallons of a memorable dry rosé by combining the skins and
pulp from a run of Zinfandel with some inexpensive white
Shasta table grapes we picked late in the season. The
relatively bland Shastas provided a high sugar content; the
Zinfandel skins and pulp, which themselves had yielded
twenty gallons of red wine in the pressing, later provided
color and flavor to the rosé, which we fermented and aged
like a white wine.

Tasting wine and asking questions — particularly at
the small wineries — is a good way of picking up an
education about wines and wine making. (It also makes an
enjoyable day's outing, if you are fortunate enough to live
near wine country. One of my favorites, though there are
many others, is the Nichelini family winery in the steep
hills northeast of Napa. Visitors gather under the massive,
forty-foot beam of an old single-beam Roman wine press in
the outdoor courtyard "tasting room," which overlooks a
small creek on the hillside below. Jim and Betty Nichelini
pour the wine — and quite generously — themselves.)

Both commercial and amateur wine makers tend to
exchange information freely. I have been invited to watch
the fall crush and fermentation in a number of Napa Valley
wineries. From the friendly brothers in the laboratory of the
Christian Brothers winery at Mont La Salle in the hills near
Napa, I learned basic tips on the difficult art of blending.

The year before, I had located 300 pounds of young, first-yield Cabernet Sauvignon grapes in Dry Creek Valley, a superb wine region just northwest of the Napa Valley. But after a year's aging, the pure Cabernet I had made was brutally rough, containing enough acid to pucker the hide of an elephant. After consultation with several commercial wine makers, I learned that pure Cabernet would settle down enough to be drinkable only after about five years of aging. Practically no one makes pure Cabernet Sauvignon — it has to be blended, generally with Petit Sirrah, the all-purpose red blending wine.

The Petit Sirrah grape itself has an interesting history in California. Because of its high yield and excellent blending qualities, it was planted heavily. During Prohibition, when many California vineyards withered and died, Petit Sirrah was planted and cultivated to make sacramental wines. It makes an excellent burgundy wine, and for decades was marketed simply as burgundy, but lately, due to the increasing sophistication of American wine drinkers, Petit Sirrah is often marketed under the varietal label and commands premium prices.

Jim Nichelini, the third-generation operator of his family winery, laughed about this. "I've been making Petit Sirrah the same way all my life," he said, "and now people want a fancy label. Funny thing is, the stores want to raise the price, so I can't fight that."

Equipment

Much of the wine-making equipment also doubles for use in making beer. With the exception of crushers and presses, which are quite expensive (but can be rented), the initial investment is modest.

- Primary fermenter: plastic, wood or crock. Wood should be lined with heavy-duty plastic bags. Seventeen pounds of grapes will yield approximately one gallon of juice; 100 pounds of grapes will therefore require a fermenter of 13-gallon capacity (to allow extra space for fermentation).

- Secondary fermenters: oak barrels, plastic or glass 5-gallon bottles (carboys). Reconditioned whiskey and wine barrels are readily available. New oak barrels, especially the French Limousin oak ones, are quite expensive. Five-gallon water bottles may be purchased quite inexpensively from water-bottling companies, which dispose of chipped or stained bottles.

- Syphon hose, hydrometer, funnel, hand corker, fermentation locks.

Red Wines

Red Wine Method

1. Sterilize all equipment with a solution of 2 ounces of potassium or sodium metabisulphite per 1 gallon of water (barrels may be sterilized by this method or by burning sulphur candles in them). Fortunately for wine and beer making, sulphur dioxide effectively kills yeast organisms and then disappears itself.

2. De-stem at least half the total amount of grapes. Leaving some stems in the "must" provides desirable tannin.

3. Crush grapes. A simple process with a crusher, but may be done by squeezing small amounts at a time by hand or by stomping a few gallons at a time in a clean plastic trash basket. Children love to do this.

4. If you wish to use Andovin or Montrachet wine yeast, dissolve 1½ teaspoons potassium or sodium metabisulphite in a small amount of warm water and stir into each 100 pounds of grapes. Let sit for 4 hours before adding yeast. Most traditional home wine makers do not bother to sterilize the "must" this way and then add Andovin and Montrachet yeast, but simply allow a natural ferment from the heavy deposits of yeast cells on the grape skins. Commercial wine makers, who cannot afford fermenting failures, follow the process outlined here. I use both methods, and have never lost a ferment due to the naturally occurring yeasts going wild or "off."

5. Measure sugar content. Strain out enough juice to fill the hydrometer jar. Specific gravity should read between 1.090 and 1.100. If sugar is low, add cane sugar. Three ounces of sugar per gallon of juice will raise the specific gravity by 0.009. If sugar is too high for a dry wine, add water. One quart of water per gallon of juice will bring the specific gravity down by 0.010.

6. Check acid. Acid-testing kits are available at wine-supply stores. Red grapes should have an acid content of 0.65 to 0.75 percent. This process, however, is not essential for the home wine maker. We know that California vinifera grapes will usually need at least 1 ounce of acid blend per 100 pounds of grapes.

7. After checking sugar and acid content, add the Andovin or Montrachet yeast (if using added-yeast method) and cover the fermenter with a clean plastic sheet, tied down. Gently push the ball of fermenting grapes (the "cap") under the juice twice daily. Ferment 3 to 5 days or until specific gravity reads 1.040.

8. *Free Run Wine:* This batch will age mellow more quickly than the second run. Tape the syphon hose to a 3- or 4-foot piece of clean doweling or wood stick. Poke this carefully through the cap to clear wine — about 2 inches off the bottom of the fermenter. Syphon juice into a plastic pail, using a plastic strainer to catch seeds, pulp or grapes. Syphon or pour the juice into secondary fermenter and attach fermentation lock. (For a few days, the active ferment will probably force juice and pulp into and out of the fermentation lock and create a mess that will have to be cleaned daily.)

When all free-run wine is off, press the pulp for second run wine. If you do not have a press, or do not wish to use a press, use the following method for second run wine.

9. *Second Run Wine:* For each gallon of juice you took off, put back 1 gallon water, 2 pounds sugar, ½ teaspoon yeast nutrient and ½ ounce acid blend. Let ferment 3 to 5 days until specific gravity reads 1.010. Syphon off juice as before, then squeeze pulp by hand through large plastic strainer.

10. Racking is syphoning juice off the "lees" or residue, in the bottom of the fermenter. Rack after 10 to 12 days into clean secondary fermenters to remove excess and dead yeast deposit. Top up (fill) fermenters with water or wine. Rack again in 2 months.

11. Bottling may be done any time after six months — earlier for Gamay Beaujolais or white wines. Two weeks before bottling, "fine" the wine by dissolving ½ teaspoon Knox gelatin in a cup of water for each 5-gallon fermenter. Boil the gelatin-water mixture for 3 minutes, allow to cool, and pour into wine. This clears the wine by carrying sediment to the bottom. When ready, syphon into bottles that have been sterilized with the basic potassium metabisulphite mixture, cork, and store on their sides.

White Wines

Within the past ten years, Oregon and Washington wine makers have begun to produce some remarkably good white wines in commercial quantities. The vinifera grapes seem to do best when planted in protected interior valleys that shelter the vines from the heavy coastal rainfall in those areas.

White wine is a bit more difficult to ferment than red because the juice must first be extracted from the grapes before the ferment. Also, fermentation should be done at a lower temperature than for reds. Homemade white wines, on the other hand, do not require the aging process of reds and may usually be drunk early the following spring.

White Wine Method

1. *Free Run White Wine:*   Press juice from crushed grapes and pour into primary fermenter. Adjust sugar and acid as for red wine. Allow the juice to settle overnight without fermentation lock — cover loosely. Rack juice into carboy and add yeast (if using a prepared yeast). Attach fermentation lock; when vigorous ferment subsides, top up with fresh juice or water. Rack in 10 days and again in 2 to 3 months. Bottle in 6 months.

2. *Second Run White Wine:* Place pressed pulp back into primary fermenter. For each gallon of juice pressed in first run, add 1 gallon water, 2 pounds sugar, ½ ounce acid blend, ½ teaspoon yeast nutrient and wine yeast. Process like second run red wine.

Note: Under no circumstances should bread yeast ever be used in wine or beer making. It will ferment the must and wort but will give a cloudy product with a noticeable yeast flavor. Many amateur wine and beer makers use bread yeast, but the loss in quality is considerable. On the other hand, the beer yeast residue left after racking beer makes a superb, tangy bread yeast!

Wines for Fun

Practically all fruit and, surprisingly enough, many vegetables make good wine. The best fruit wines seem to come from plums, blackberries and loganberries, apples, peaches and elderberries. The following recipes for elderberry wine, apple cider and wine, plum wine, dandelion wine, and an unusual recipe for beet wine, should get you started.

Elderberries make a fine dry, dessert or port wine, depending on the process one uses. I have served, at festive Thanksgiving and Christmas dinners, a three-year-old elderberry wine that rivalled the best of clarets.

Both dried and fresh elderberries make good wine, but I have found that for some reason dried elderberries make a better one. Elderberries are easily dried in the sun — it takes a week or less — and may be stored indefinitely in tightly sealed jars in a cool, dry place.

Elderberry Wine
(1 gallon)

6 ounces dried elderberries
1 pound raisins
1 gallon water
2 pounds white sugar
½ teaspoon yeast nutrient
3 teaspoons acid blend
1 Campden tablet (or ½ cup potassium metabisulphite
    solution; see page 215)
1 teaspoon ascorbic acid
Wine yeast

Chop raisins. Mix all except yeast in primary
fermenter; add yeast when must is cool (70° to 75° F). Cover
with plastic sheet tied down. Stir daily; ferment for 5 to 7
days, then syphon through plastic strainer into a plastic
bucket and pour into gallon jug. Attach fermentation lock;
rack after 1 month and again in 3 months. When wine is
clear, add 1 Campden tablet (which stops fermentation) and
1 teaspoon ascorbic acid (which prevents oxidation) per
gallon; bottle. Age 9 months.

Apples make both a bracing, sparkling cider (with
alcoholic content of about 6 percent) and, when fermented
with care, a light, quite dry white wine. Depending on the
variety of apple, you will need 14 to 16 pounds of fruit for one
gallon of juice. As always in the case of ciders, a blend of
apples gives the best results. Windfalls and otherwise
damaged apples are fine for cider and wine. Red and Golden
Delicious, Lodi and other soft summer apples yield a
poor-quality wine.

Apple Cider

1 gallon fresh apple juice
Sugar to specific gravity 1.060
½ teaspoon pectic enzyme powder
½ teaspoon acid blend
¼ teaspoon grape tannin
¼ teaspoon yeast energizer
1 Campden tablet
Andovin or Montrachet wine yeast

Crush apples. If you do not have access to a crusher or press, chop apples into small pieces and mash with potato masher. Put crushed apples in a nylon mesh or cheesecloth bag. Dissolve crushed Campden tablet in small amount of water and add to crushed apples. Press pulp as dry as possible, squeezing the bag. Let juice settle overnight in covered primary fermenter.

Next day, syphon carefully to remove juice from apple solids. Adjust sugar for specific gravity of 1.060. Add all other ingredients, including yeast. Ferment in primary fermenter 3 to 5 days or until specific gravity is 1.020. Syphon into gallon jug(s) or carboy and attach fermentation locks.

Rack after about 3 weeks when specific gravity is 1.000, and add 1 teaspoon per gallon ascorbic acid (antioxidant). When clear and stable, syphon into primary fermenter. For each gallon of cider dissolve 2 ounces white sugar in a little cider and stir gently. Syphon cider into bottles and cap with crown caps. Age 2 to 3 months.

This recipe may be made in multiples. A 5-gallon batch will fill 2½ cases of returnable beer bottles.

Apple Wine

This is a dry wine. The recipe is for one gallon but may be made in multiples.

6 pounds apples
2 pounds white sugar
1 Campden tablet
1 teaspoon yeast nutrient
½ ounce acid blend
½ teaspoon pectic enzyme powder
¼ teaspoon grape tannin
½ teaspoon Knox gelatin
½ teaspoon ascorbic acid
1 gallon water
Wine yeast

If possible, crush apples, press and use just the juice. Otherwise, chop apples fine and put all ingredients except yeast in primary fermenter and mix well. Add yeast, cover with plastic sheet and ferment 4 to 5 days or until specific gravity is 1.040. Strain out fruit and press or squeeze. Syphon into gallon jugs or carboy and attach fermentation locks. Rack after 3 weeks and again in 3 months. Fine with gelatin (see page 217); when wine is clear and stable, bottle. When bottling, add ¼ teaspoon ascorbic acid per gallon to prevent oxidation. Age 1 year.

Plum Wine

Plums are cheap and plentiful throughout California in the summer — indeed, tons of them go to waste in vacant lots and abandoned orchards. This plum wine recipe produces a soft, fruity but remarkably dry wine. It is, of course, the base for the powerful, stinging refined Yugoslavian plum brandy known as *slivovitz*.

2½ pounds ripe plums
2½ pounds white sugar
  ½ teaspoon pectic enzyme powder
  ½ teaspoon yeast nutrient
  1 Campden tablet
1½ teaspoon acid blend
  ½ teaspoon Knox gelatin
  ½ teaspoon ascorbic acid
  1 gallon water
Wine yeast

Remove stones and crush plums. Put all ingredients except yeast into primary fermenter. Heat the water and stir in to dissolve sugar. Cover with plastic sheet. When must is cool (70° to 75° F), add yeast. Stir the must daily. Ferment 5 to 6 days or until specific gravity is 1.040. Strain out fruit pulp and press or squeeze. Syphon into gallon jugs or carboys and attach fermentation locks. Rack after 3 weeks and again in 3 months. When wine is clear and stable, fine with gelatin and bottle when settled. Add ¼ teaspoon per gallon ascorbic acid and bottle. Age 1 year.

Dandelion Wine

I am not particularly enamored of dandelion wine, perhaps because of the sweetish, heavy traditional recipes so many folks use in the Midwest. But it is certainly inexpensive and fun to make. This recipe produces a light, quite dry wine. It is for 1 gallon and may be made in multiples.

6 cups dandelion petals (preferably picked *before* the plant
    becomes heavily mature)
2 pounds white sugar
1 pound Thompson Seedless raisins
3 teaspoons acid blend
1 Campden tablet
½ teaspoon yeast energizer
¼ teaspoon grape tannin
½ teaspoon Knox gelatin
¼ teaspoon ascorbic acid
1 gallon water
Wine yeast

Use only the petals of the dandelion plant. Chop raisins and put all ingredients except yeast in primary fermenter. Pour gallon of hot water over ingredients and stir to dissolve sugar. Add yeast when must is cool (70° to 75° F). Ferment for 3 days, strain, syphon into gallon jugs or carboy and attach fermentation lock. Rack after 3 weeks and again in 3 months. Keep topped up with water if necessary. When wine is clear and stable, fine with gelatin. Bottle when clear, adding ¼ teaspoon ascorbic acid per gallon to prevent oxidation. Age 6 months.

The following recipe was passed on to me by a friend who got it from a friend who found it written on a stained scrap of paper in an abandoned house outside Aberdeen, Washington. The recipe is given as found, Germanic spelling and all. It is the basic beet and parsnip wine method developed many centuries ago in Middle Europe. Floating the yeast on a slice of toast not only distributes it well, but the toast also imparts a nice color to light wines.

Beet Wine

"12 beets kochen in 1 gallon of water. Strain. Then add 3 partz sugar, 2 slices of toast, spreat with 1 yeast cake. Let stand until fermented, then bottle." (By substituting wine yeast for the yeast cake, and by reading 2 pounds of sugar for "3 partz sugar," I have made a tasty, dry red wine.)

WINTER

Winter Fires

Sometimes the land itself burns
here in the California Delta.

(The leveed land, a hundred centuries
flowing of the San Joaquin, the Sacramento, the
Mokelumne, Tuolumne and Consumnes.)

Land so rich it burns:
an amazing thing!
spongy black peat
dry before November rains.

Farmers fire the levee-bound fields
orange flame eddies like
Delta backwaters
ashing pale yellow rice straw,
the black and scored tangle of
exhausted asparagus.

Here on the bank of Steamboat Slough
gray-wool November clouds
blanket life—
the Pacific-cold gale
tears at our driftwood fire.

Behind us, as we tend crayfish traps
Miner Slough rustles darkly by
above our heads.

Quiet across the driftwood fire
we watch shapes of ourselves
rise to join the blue-haze
Delta air—
winter-blue air
thickened by burning fields and land
and the fires of the heart.

Oregon Winter

"It's God's blessing, Dimmudy, you won't have to spend another drafty Christmas freezing to death in this worn-out old house."

The gaunt, white Oregon-gothic farmhouse shook and groaned under the force of the winter storm. The lace curtains in the parlor billowed slightly from the chill drafts. The diffused yellow light of the coal-oil mantle lamps, spreading resolutely, just managed to fill the room. It softened the features of the American travelers in Paris whom grandson John-Robert was studying through Dimmudy's Stereopticon.

Pushing her mail-order spectacles higher on her nose, Dimmudy gazed noncommittally at her daughter, then returned her attention to the intricate patching of the worn Morning Star quilt spread across her lap. The oak rocker creaked as she worked.

"There's always been things enough in this house to keep me warm on a winter night, Esther," Dimmudy said, her 79-year-old voice as clear as a school girl's. The firelight glowed warmly on the thick, iron-gray braids of hair wound around her head. "Memories is what, and the care of Jonathan's hands carving that woodwork and fittin' rafters. No crackerbox house in town is going to keep me warm."

"Dimmudy," said Esther, "we've been all over that." Because she was the youngest of ten, Esther had always been the scrappiest. Now she was spokeswoman for the eight remaining children. The glossy black braids of hair, piled high on her head, gave Esther a faintly regal air.

"You may not think that house in La Grande is going to keep you warm," she continued firmly, "but it'll sure as rain keep you alive. It worries all our minds, you out here alone. Come the thaw in spring, there's two months you can't get in nor out of that mud-rut lane to the county road. Nothing to do but draw water, read the Henry Field seed catalog and hope you don't break a hip, or worse. And Alf Hicks, he ain't yet paid you last year's shares on his barley out of the Spring Creek forty. You could freeze to a chunk for all that Hicks clan could care!"

Dimmudy carefully folded the Morning Star quilt in her lap. She laid it on the cobbler's bench by the rocker and picked up another quilt, its design only a faint pattern of linked circles. She turned to the twelve-year-old, who had tired of the Stereopticon and now lay on the floor, dreamily watching the red whorls of the oak fire and wondering if the squirrels, curled with red tails covering their faces, felt the Christmas blizzard in their hollow oak trees.

"You, John-Robert, I hope you have this Wedding Ring quilt someday," she said. "When we brought it from Indiana in '79, it kept me and Jonathan warm many a winter night in that cabin we built yonder. Now why don't you use those young legs, boy, and fetch that Blue Willow pitcher of buttermilk from the safe?"

John-Robert sprang to his feet, went through the tidy,

yellow kitchen and entered the unheated pantry. He loved
the cool, yeasty bread-and-pie fragrances of the tall oak
"safe," zinc-lined to keep out bugs and mice. Between the
safe and the springhouse, where butter and sweet milk were
kept, Dimmudy had never needed a refrigerator.

"Bring that bowl of hazelnuts on the kitchen table,
too, John-Robert," Dimmudy's clear voice floated through
the big kitchen. With Dimmudy's farm and house sold right
after Christmas, John-Robert wondered if he would ever
again hunt hazelnuts like buried treasure in the rifts of
golden-brown leaves under the head-high bushes. He
remembered Lukey, his 13-year-old and therefore wiser
cousin, had showed him how to find whole quarts of
hazelnuts that the squirrels had stored in leaf-lined burrows
around the roots of the hazelbrush. They had spent
wood-smelling October afternoons robbing squirrels in the
patch up the hill from Dimmudy's half-acre truck garden.

"And with no woods to run," Dimmudy was saying
when John-Robert reentered the parlor, "how's that
city-bred boy going to learn things such like finding wild
spring greens?"

"Dimmudy," Esther said, exasperated, with a look at
John-Robert, "we ought to be thinking about our Christmas
now. John-Robert will remember this last Christmas here
joyfully, knowin' you're going to be in good hands in town."

There was a loud snow-stomping on the veranda. The
stained-glass front door, propelled by the wind, slammed
open. It was Uncle Archer and Aunt Emaline, Dimmudy's
oldest daughter, with four of John-Robert's cousins trailing
along behind.

"Merry Christmas, everybody!" shouted Uncle Archer. An auctioneer, he shouted at everyone. "Dimmudy! Them lane ruts of yours is frozen arn-hard, enough to tear the wheel offen an A-Model! I'll sure be glad when you're livin' on city-paved streets!"

Lying again before the fire, John-Robert looked over his shoulder at Dimmudy. She seemed not to have heard the noisy entrance. Head bent, she was gently stroking the Wedding Ring quilt covering her lap. The firelight burnished two streams of tears on her cheeks. She seemed to John-Robert to be staring into the distance at something about to be lost, something she could not with words share.

Watching her, John-Robert decided that he and Lukey hadn't been fair to the squirrels now curled up in their tree dens. He got up, preparing to greet his cousins. Next year, if he went nut hunting, he would pick his own.

Making Bread

The novelty of the new is an American weakness that often leads to distressing lapses of taste. During my farm boyhood, the pungent, mouth-watering aroma of baking salt-rising "light bread" filled almost every household two or three times a week. We lived in isolated hill country where folks had neither the convenience of freezers nor easy access to town. When the counties improved the farm-to-market roads, however, presliced, doughy store-bought bread quickly became a favorite farm luxury, and bread making at home went into decline. By the end of World War II, many farm families had forgotten entirely the hearty taste and firm texture of homemade bread.

Now the trend has reversed, and more and more people, city and country alike, are rediscovering the delights of fresh bread made at home. The reasons are obvious: First, it tastes and feels better. Homemade bread has a rich, nourishing flavor and a substantial texture that a mass-producing commercial bakery just can't approach. Second, nothing goes into your bread that you don't put there. You are assured of the wholesomeness of your ingredients, and your bread will not need dough conditioners, preservatives, or enriching with vitamins. Finally, there is the satisfaction of having proven your self-reliance once again. Instead of relying on the supermarket, you will have done something for yourself — and done it better.

Some hopeful home bakers are discouraged by an initial failure or two. Others are put off at the start by the seeming complexity of the task or the time it takes. Let none of these hold you back. Bread making is really simplicity itself. Everyone who makes bread has had loaves that failed (or succeeded marginally), dough that refuses to rise (a fault in the yeast) or loaves with an air pocket under the top crust (because they have risen too much in the pans). Such failures are greatly minimized, however, once you understand the natural processes that create a loaf of bread. The two most critical processes, which I'll discuss separately below, are kneading the dough and maintaining the proper rising temperature for the yeast: Both are easily mastered. As for the time involved, it is not really that much. Besides mixing the dough, kneading and forming the loaves are the only other parts of the process that require your active involvement. While the bread is rising and baking, you are free to drink tea, read a magazine, or putter in the garden. Once you've tasted the results of your afternoon's work, you'll consider the time well spent.

(Many people are even finding that the high-priced "convenience" of prepackaged baking mixes is a dubious advantage in speed. With a little practice, an enterprising cook can prepare homemade biscuits, pancakes, shortcakes and cookies from scratch just about as quickly as one who uses prepackaged materials.)

Kneading   Practically all bread dough must be kneaded firmly for at least ten minutes — until the dough has a satiny sheen and firm consistency and no longer sticks to hands or bread board.

Turn the dough out onto a well-floured board. If the dough is too sticky to handle, flour your hands and sprinkle flour on the dough as you knead. Begin kneading by cupping the right or left hand slightly (whichever is more comfortable) and pushing from the center of the dough outward with the heel of your hand. Be firm but gentle. When extended, fold the dough back toward you, turn it a quarter-turn and repeat.

Some people like to knead with their knuckles; probably someone somewhere throws an elbow in here and there. For most people, I think, the heel-of-the-hand method brings more body weight into the process, which ensures a smoother final texture to the bread. Do whatever is comfortable for you, but be gentle: never smack, throw or hit the dough.

Knead rhythmically. It is a strenuous activity and your breath may begin to come short, your arms tire. Let the *rhythm* of the process carry you through to your second wind. There will be plenty of time to relax, read, drink tea or prune your house plants while the dough is rising.

Proper Rising   Most basic homemade breads benefit from being allowed to rise twice before the final rising in the pans. The second rising process usually takes only half the time of the first.

Proper rising depends on proper treatment of the yeast. To test the yeast and to give it a vigorous start, always "proof" it before mixing the dough. To proof yeast, put it in one-half cup of warm (never hot) water along with the sugar called for in the recipe (or at least a half-tablespoon, if none is called for). Within a few minutes the yeast will begin visibly working and the mixture will triple in size.

Unless the kitchen temperature is 85°, place the rising bread on an oven rack over a bowl of hot water, cover bread loosely with a towel or cloth and close the oven door. Replenish the hot water for each successive rising. This ensures steady, vigorous growth.

When a rising is complete gently punch the bread down with the knuckles (actually, it is "pushing" rather than "punching," though the latter word is invariably used in bread-making instructions).

The variety of homemade breads the world over is limited only by imagination and ingredients available. The recipes given here are American standards — the breads baked in America from colonial times to the present, brought West by pioneers and even, in the case of sourdough bread, one that is a native to the West Coast.

The Breads

Buttermilk Bread

This is my favorite bread recipe. Buttermilk bread has a texture, taste and crust very like sourdough, but the mixing and baking process is much simpler. It makes a crusty, firm-textured loaf or rolls that are yet resiliently soft in the center. The loaves slice well and do not crumble.

2 packages dry yeast
1 tablespoon sugar
1 tablespoon salt
3 tablespoons melted butter, shortening or vegetable oil
2 cups buttermilk
6 (approx.) cups flour (preferably unbleached)

Combine yeast, sugar and ½ cup warm water to proof the yeast. Mix salt, buttermilk, melted butter in a large bowl. Allow yeast to proof 10 minutes, then add to bowl, along with 3 cups of the flour. Mix with a large fork or spoon. Gradually mix in remainder of the flour.

Turn onto floured board and knead 10 minutes. Let dough rest a few minutes, then place in a greased bowl, turning once to grease top of dough. Cover with towel and place bowl in oven over bowl of hot water. Let rise for 1 to 1½ hours, or until indentation made with finger does not pop back out.

Turn out on floured board and knead lightly for 2 minutes. Divide dough by cutting gently with sharp knife and form into loaves that will fill bread pans ½ to ⅔ full. Seal the ends of the loaves by turning under and pinching dough. Put dough into greased baking pans, return to oven, cover with towel, and let rise again over hot water until it has doubled in size.

Bake loaves at 375° for about 40 minutes — until loaf gives out a firm, hollow sound when rapped with knuckles. Turn loaf out on wire rack. If bottom is soft return loaf pan to oven and bake another 5 to 10 minutes.

For best crust and easy slicing, let loaves cool thoroughly and "cure" well in open air for 2 hours.

Buttermilk Bread Rolls

Use the same recipe and process as for Buttermilk Bread up to the step of shaping the loaves. Gently roll the dough out to a thickness of 2 inches with a rolling pin, then cut dough into 2-inch squares. Fold edges of rolls under and place in greased pie pans so they are not quite touching. Return to oven and let rise over hot water until double in bulk. Bake in 375° oven for about 20 minutes or until well-browned. Turn out on wire rack to cool. These rolls reheat to original crispness in a 350° oven. Excellent for keeping in freezer and heating for meals. Also the perfect roll to serve with Barbecued Brisket (page 97).

Salt-Rising Bread

Like Sourdough (page 248), salt-rising bread undergoes an overnight fermentation process that gives real bite and authority to the baked bread. The famous West Coast sourdough bread undoubtedly descended from Gold Rush variations on the ages-old process of perpetuating indefinitely a "starter" or natural yeast for salt-rising and basic white breads. My maternal grandmother baked regularly from a starter she had maintained for over thirty years. Contrary to what the name suggests, salt-rising bread contains only a very small amount of salt. Healthfully enough, it does not call for sugar or fat, except what is already in the milk. This bread should be begun the evening before it is to be baked.

The evening before:

4 tablespoons boiling water
½ teaspoon salt
½ cup flour

Into a large bowl pour boiling water over flour and salt; mix to a stiff paste. Cover bowl with a towel and place on a rack in oven over hot water overnight.
The next day:

2 cups warm milk
½ teaspoon salt
4 cups flour
1 package dry yeast proofed in ½ cup water and 1 teaspoon
    sugar (sugar may be omitted)

Mix these ingredients into the overnight starter. Dough will be somewhat soupy. Cover bowl and place on rack in oven over a bowl of hot water and let stand for about 1½ hours until batter rises. Then stir in an additional 2½ cups of flour (save out ½ cup of flour to knead in if necessary to avoid getting too stiff a dough). Knead for 10 minutes; dough will not have the satiny sheen of regular bread but will be flexible. Place dough in greased bowls, turning to lightly grease top, and return to oven to rise over bowl of hot water. When doubled in bulk, punch down and form into loaves. Let rise in greased bread pans over hot water in oven for 1 hour. Bake in 450° oven for approximately 20 minutes, or until loaf gives out a hollow sound when rapped with knuckles on the bottom.

Indian, or Southern Gentleman, Cornbread

As a small child in the San Fernando Valley near Los Angeles, I used to swap my turkey and roast beef sandwiches for slabs of this cornbread a Cherokee Indian schoolmate frequently carried for lunch — and years later enjoyed the same crusty cornbread in the homes of Cherokee Indian friends in and around Tahlequah; Oklahoma. A close friend from South Carolina once prepared and served the same recipe, claiming that it was the true "Southern Gentleman" cornbread.

At any rate, it is the genuine article: inexpensive, easy to make, basically nutritious, nuttier and crustier than the sugar-softened cornbreads found in many recipe books. The preheated, cast-iron skillet ensures a golden brown, thick-crusted cornbread.

1 cup yellow or white cornmeal
½ cup flour
1½ teaspoons salt
1 teaspoon sugar
3 tablespoons shortening
½ cup boiling water
½ cup milk
1 egg
1½ teaspoon baking powder

Mix cornmeal, flour, salt, sugar and shortening in a bowl. Cut shortening into meal with pastry cutter or two knives until mixture is granulated. Stir in boiling water. Add cold milk; stir well. When batter is at room temperature, mix in egg and then baking powder, beating briskly. Preheat lightly greased cast-iron skillet or "corn-stick" griddles in 425° oven. Pour in batter and bake until well-browned (about 20 minutes).

Sourdough Baking

From Sutter's Mill and Dutch Flat in the California gold rush country to the Klondike in Alaska, miners and mountain men made do with what they had. As a result, they gave the world one of the tastiest breads — not to mention rolls, pancakes and waffles — ever baked. So while everybody is enjoying the sweets of modern life, let's not forget the distinctive, zesty flavor of sourdough.

As I have learned over the years of serious study of the art of beer making, yeasts are among the most complicated — and still mysterious — of life forms. And it is the yeast strains that come into existence in sourdough starter that impart the distinctive, subtle flavors to sourdough breads. These strains may change over a period of time — thus changing the flavor — increasing the vigor or sometimes inexplicably dying out. (San Francisco sourdough bakeries, for instance, keep different age-strains of their starter on hand to avoid the possibility of a yeast strain "going off," as they say.)

In an earlier America, all home-baked bread was made with starter rather than packaged yeast. (In fact, I know of someone who is still using and replenishing a starter that came across the country in a covered wagon.) What makes sourdough different is the overnight (or at least six-hour) fermentation period allowed for the basic dough. You can get sourdough starter from a friend or from some bakeries on the West Coast. However, it is also easy to start your own from scratch.

Sourdough Starter

3 cups flour
1 package dry yeast
1½ cups lukewarm water (110° to 115°)

Mix yeast until dissolved in the water; pour over flour in a mixing bowl. With a large fork or spoon stir the mixture well, then beat vigorously to dissolve all lumps and make mixture smooth. Cover with a towel and set bowl on rack in oven over bowl of hot water and leave for 24 hours, replenishing the hot water when it gets cool. This makes about 4 cups. After using starter you need, return the rest to a glass jar or crock with tight lid and keep in the refrigerator. The starter put back should be used and replenished (as shown below) at least every two weeks; the more often it is used, the better.

Sourdough Bread

1 cup sourdough starter
2 cups warm water
2 cups flour

Mix well with large fork or spoon. Batter should be thick but not too hard to stir. Cover bowl with towel and place on rack in oven over bowl of hot water overnight. Next day, take out 1 cup of this mixture and reserve as future starter — add to starter mixture already in refrigerator or store by itself in jar or crock with tight lid.

1 egg
1 teaspoon salt
2 tablespoons sugar
3 tablespoons melted butter or shortening

Mix thoroughly. Add enough additional flour (2 to 4 cups) to make a firm bread dough. Flour may be kneaded in. Knead 10 minutes on a floured board until dough has a satin sheen. Cut with a large, sharp knife into loaf-size pieces and place in greased bread pans or coffee cans. Dough will easily triple in bulk, so amount needed will depend on size of baking tins. Place pans of dough on rack in oven over bowl of hot water and let rise for about 1½ hours or until double or triple in bulk. Allow to rise once only. Bake in preheated 350° oven approximately 45 minutes or until golden brown and loaf has pulled away from sides of pan. Turn out on wire rack to cool. Yields 3 small or 2 large loaves.

Sourdough Rolls

1 tablespoon sugar
1 package dry yeast
1½ cups warm water
1 cup sourdough starter
3½ to 4 cups flour
1 tablespoon melted butter or shortening

Proof yeast with ½ cup lukewarm water and sugar. Pour yeast mixture over sourdough starter in large mixing bowl. Add remaining cup of lukewarm water. With a large fork or spoon, stir in 2 cups of flour and mix well. Cover with towel and place on rack in oven over bowl of hot water. Let rise for 2 hours or until dough doubles in volume. Stir briefly with large fork or spoon and place 1 cup back in refrigerator in tight jar or with previous starter. Gradually add 1½ cups flour to mixture in the bowl, stirring vigorously. Add flour until dough is firm but not dry. Knead for 10 minutes on floured board. Place dough in greased bowl, turning to grease top, and return to rack in oven over bowl of hot water. Let rise for about 1 hour or until dough doubles in volume.

Grease a cookie sheet. Turn dough out on board after punching down with a single blow of the fist. Gently flatten to 2-inch thickness with a rolling pin and cut dough into 12 equal squares with large, sharp knife. Shape gently into balls and flatten slightly, arranging about 2 inches apart on cookie sheet. Bake in 375° oven 20 minutes or until golden and crisp.

Sourdough pancakes are nothing like the bland, cakey product that comes from many boxed mixes. They are thin, funky-yeasty, golden-brown and crisp around the edges. When frying, they fill the house with a baking smell that guarantees a ravenous breakfast appetite.

Sourdough Pancakes

Mix a batch of the overnight-fermenting second starter described in the Sourdough Bread recipe. Store back 1 cup, as before.

In the morning, mix thoroughly with the overnight starter:

2 eggs
1 teaspoon salt
1 teaspoon baking soda
3 tablespoons sugar
3 tablespoons melted butter or shortening

Fry on hot, well-greased griddle, turning when raw side is bubbly. Makes 8 to 12 pancakes.

Sourdough Waffles

Use the pancake recipe, but separate eggs and fold stiffly beaten whites into the mixture.

Making Cheese

Anyone who has ever tasted the robust, full-bodied cheddars and cottage cheeses made by home cheese makers marvels at the natural good flavor of these products. It is true, there are some excellent American cheeses made commercially in Oregon, Wisconsin and New York, but the cheese made right in your kitchen can easily match the finest of these. With the prices of even the most common store cheeses climbing toward $3 a pound, this almost-lost art appears to be enjoying a renaissance in American homes. By infusing mold cultures in the form of small amounts of imported or specialty cheeses, the home cheese maker can even make anything from Limburger to Liederkranz, Port Salut to Gruyère.

Cheese making, to those who haven't done it, will probably be the most intriguing and mysterious — and can therefore perhaps be the most satisfying — of all the processes discussed in this book. Where the wine or beer maker has recourse to the hydrometer to scientifically measure just how things are going, the cheese maker, it appears, can only wait and see. In reality, of course, there is no mystery. It is simply a matter of controlling the action of nature's yeasts, enzymes, microbes and, in some cases, molds. Milk is fermented and curdled (I have never known anyone who wanted to make cheese who was unable to get over his or her initial queasiness about this), the whey (light liquid) is drained off, and the remaining curd is cooked, pressed, salted and aged. As simple as that.

Equipment

As with beer and wine making, the equipment for making cheese may be purchased at specialty stores (at considerable expense), picked up at garage sales or flea markets, or constructed rather simply. You'll need:

- A 6- to 8-quart cooking pot of stainless steel or enamel
- A larger kettle to hold the cooking pot in a double-boiler arrangement
- Dairy thermometer, or one that reads on a scale from 80° to 212°. (I use an industrial thermometer from a cannery, purchased for $1.50 at a flea market. It is calibrated to read at one-degree intervals from 60° to 220° and effectively shows the temperatures of beer wort, wine must and cheese milk.)
- Long-handled spoon
- Knife with long, stainless-steel blade
- Colander
- Cheesecloth
- Cheese hoop (see below)
- Deep pan or bowl
- Cheese press

Cheese Press   A cheese press is a magnificently simple and direct piece of technology, easily constructed from scrap wood or from lumber costing about $2. Because of its unique, wood-grained simplicity, it *looks* good, and I cannot resist the temptation to leave the cheese press out in the kitchen, where it makes a fine emergency cutting board (and often elicits a puzzled, admiring query from kitchen visitors). As the illustration shows, the press consists of a base board, a similar-size top, or "follower", two dowels for the follower to ride up and down on, and four common bricks. The dowels may be broomsticks. They are glued into holes drilled in the base board. The holes in the follower must be larger than the dowels so that it can be moved up and down easily. Some cheese makers like to drill small holes in the base board for the expressed whey to drain out, but this is not necessary (see page 269).

Cheese Hoop   The cheese hoop, the mold that holds the curds when they are put into the press, can be made from a one-pound coffee can or a large fruit-juice can. In this case the follower is the can lid, cut out so that it fits inside the can; the edges should be filed smooth. The curds are put into the cheesecloth-lined can (which has holes punched in the bottom for draining the whey), a glass is inverted over the lid and the rig is set into the press.

A folded dish towel or similar-size piece of cotton cloth may also be used as a hoop (see Cheddar Cheese, page 270). Commercial cheese makers use large wooden hoops; you can make a small one from thin, pliable wood, but it is a difficult process.

As in beer and wine making, cleanliness is absolutely essential. Unwanted microorganisms thrive in smidgens of left-over milk. All cheese-making equipment should be scrubbed with hot, soapy water immediately after use and rinsed with boiling water. The cheesecloth should be washed the same way and briefly boiled in clear water.

Ingredients

There are four ingredients in cheese: (1) milk; (2) a starter (buttermilk, yoghurt or sour milk), which provides bacteria that produce acid; (3) a coagulant (rennet) which quickens the separation of curds and whey; and (4) salt.

Milk   Pasteurized whole milk, skim milk and instant nonfat dry milk are all used in cheese making. The better the quality of milk the better the cheese. I am fortunate enough to live in an area served by a local Sonoma County dairy that sells nothing but all-Guernsey milk, a superb milk that makes an outstanding cheese. Goat's milk may be used in any cheese recipe; it provides a subtly different flavor than cow's milk.

Starter　Buttermilk is the most convenient starter, but yoghurt and sour milk work equally well. Use only the freshest cultured buttermilk, preferably without salt or preservatives. (Salt, because it slows or stops fermentation, is a necessary control and preserving agent later in the process.)

Rennet　An enzyme processed chiefly from sheep stomachs, rennet gives the cheese maker more control over the process by quickening the coagulation of the curds. We can make cheese without rennet, just by using buttermilk starter, but the curdling process takes as long as 48 hours. This is perfectly all right for small-curd cottage cheese, which is eaten fresh, but for cured and aged cheeses the long curdling process invites visits from unwanted molds and bacteria that can cause a ropy, bitter or fruity cured cheese. Rennet is available in tablet form in many drug stores and supermarkets. Junket tablets, which are rennet, will work in cheese making; junket *powder* will not.

American rennet supplies all during my lifetime seem to come from Charles Hansen's Laboratory, Inc., 9015 Maple Street, Milwaukee, Wisconsin 53214. They are very cooperative in filling individual orders. Each bottle of Hansen's Cheese Rennet Tablets comes with a helpful brochure explaining the cheese-making process and a recipe for a simple, delicious Hard Cheese (see Cheddar Cheese, page 266). Hansen's also provides cheese coloring, although I don't bother with it. Cheddars without coloring are a pale, whitish yellow, but have more flavor than the colored commercial product.

Salt　Any salt will do, but coarse kosher works best because it dissolves more slowly and is more fully absorbed. Salt improves the flavor of cheese, preserves it, and controls the secondary fermentation of aged cheeses.

The Basic Process

There are nine basic steps in making cheese, which I've listed here for general information. Detailed instructions for each step will be given as it is encountered in the recipes.

1. Curing or ripening the milk by adding buttermilk, yoghurt or sour milk and heating to 86° F.
2. Curdling the milk by adding rennet and allowing to stand in a warm, draft-free place until firm curds form (about 1 hour)
3. Cutting the curd
4. Cooking the curds by slowly raising the heat and holding until curds grow firm
5. Draining whey from the curds
6. Salting the curds
7. Hooping the curds and pressing the mass into cheese
8. Drying and turning the cheese
9. Curing and aging the cheese

The recipes given here are those functional, hearty cheeses most commonly served on the table. These recipes ascend in order from soft, fresh cheeses through semifirm Muenster, to the harder cheddars and finally the brick-hard dried Parmesan.

Small Curd Cottage Cheese

When I was a boy, there was always a cheesecloth bag of cottage cheese curd hanging over the kitchen sink. Since we had a cow or cows wherever we lived, freshly dressed cottage cheese was always available. Homemade cottage cheese has a much zestier flavor than the commercial product.

This recipe yields about 1½ pounds and takes one hour to process, about twelve hours for curdling.

1 gallon skim milk
½ cup instant nonfat dry milk powder
1 cup buttermilk
2 to 3 tablespoons milk, sweet or sour cream (optional)
Salt

1. Pour milk into the smaller kettle and add instant nonfat milk powder. Place in water in larger pot, a double-boiler arrangement, and heat to 86° F.

2. Hold at 86° F or at warm room temperature overnight, about 12 hours, until mixture forms a curd that pulls away from the sides of the kettle.

3. Test curd for firmness as follows (this process is a step in *all* cheese making): Make the "clean-break" test by poking the index finger on an angle into the curd to the first knuckle. Gently lift a hunk of curd with the finger — it should break cleanly from the mass before falling apart. In this cottage cheese, however, made without rennet, the curd may never become solid enough to break cleanly. Go ahead when curd is fairly firm.

4. Cut the curd into ½-inch pieces. Again, cutting the curd is a basic step in all cheese making. Using a knife with a blade long enough to reach the bottom of the curd, make ½-inch cuts through the curd; then turn the kettle ¼-turn and make ½-inch cuts again. Then, holding the knife at a 45-degree angle, make ½-inch diagonal cuts through the curd. Repeat, turning the kettle ½-turn so the second diagonal cuts are at right angles to the first ones. This should cut the curd mass into even ½-inch chunks.

5. Let the cut curds stand at 86° F for 30 minutes while the whey separates.

6. Cook the curds slowly in a double-boiler arrangement until temperature reaches 100° to 104° F. Stir gently, breaking up any large chunks you missed in the cutting. Hold at this temperature for approximately 30 minutes. (In the double-boiler arrangement, the curds and whey will normally remain at this temperature with the heat off.)

7. As soon as the curds are firm, pour mixture into a cheesecloth-lined colander over a kettle to catch the whey. (The whey may be used later to make a delicately flavored Ricotta cheese, see page 272, or may be used in the place of water or milk in making bread. Whey may be frozen until it is needed.)

8. Season to taste with salt and refrigerate. Before serving, dress with whole milk, sour or sweet cream for a creamier cheese.

Large Curd Cottage Cheese

This is a milder, less acid cheese than the small curd, but it is prepared the same way with the exception of adding rennet, which curdles the milk mixture more quickly.

1 gallon skim milk
½ cup instant nonfat dry milk powder
1 cup buttermilk
¼ rennet tablet
2 to 3 tablespoons whole milk, sweet or sour cream
    (optional)
Salt

1. Mix skim milk and milk powder and heat to 86° F in the double-boiler arrangement. Stir in buttermilk.

2. Dissolve ¼ rennet tablet in 2 tablespoons cold water and add to mixture. Stir in thoroughly.

3. Let the milk mixture stand in the double-boiler arrangement undisturbed for 3 to 5 hours.

4. Make the clean-break test; when curd is firm, cut into ½-inch pieces, using method described for Small Curd Cottage Cheese (page 260).

5. Replace kettle of curds in the double-boiler arrangement and keep at 86° F for 30 minutes to firm the curds.

Note: In this process of heating the curds, and at all times, the heat must be manipulated very carefully by turning the burner off and on. Never overcook; overcooked curds turn very quickly into something like shriveled pencil-erasers!

6. Slowly (about 5 degrees every 10 minutes) raise the temperature of the curds to between 100° and 104° F.

7. Hold the curds at this temperature for about 30 minutes. Squeeze a few curds gently in your hand; if they still crumble apart, gradually raise the heat to between 110° and 115° at the same rate as given previously. When a few curds squeeze together and remain firm, remove from heat and skim off as much whey as possible.

8. Pour curds into cheesecloth-lined colander and allow to drain thoroughly, then salt to taste and refrigerate.

9. After cheese has chilled, dress with 2 to 3 tablespoons whole milk, sweet or sour cream.

Brick Cheese

Brick, like Cheddar, is a sturdy, flavorful all-American cheese. This cheese may be eaten fresh or aged for three months for a tangy flavor.

1 gallon whole milk
1 cup buttermilk
1 rennet tablet

1. Pour buttermilk into milk and stir well. Heat milk mixture to 86° F in double-boiler arrangement. Hold at this temperature for an hour. Crush rennet tablet and dissolve in 2 tablespoons cold water; stir into milk mixture thoroughly.

2. Maintain 86° F until firm curd develops (40 minutes to 1 hour). Test curd with clean-break test. Cut curd into ½-inch cubes as for Small Curd Cottage Cheese (page 264). Stir gently on and off for 30 minutes while slowly raising temperature to 115°F. Hold at this temperature until curd is springy and does not crumble when pinched in fingers.

3. With a slotted spoon, dip curd out of whey into cheese hoop (the cheesecloth-lined coffee can or the "bandage" hoop described in Equipment, page 256. Poke holes from the inside out in the coffee can bottom and lid to facilitate draining.) Turn the hoop upside down several times at approximately 30-minute intervals (don't worry about exact times during this simple draining process).

4. Put the cheese-filled hoop in the cheese press and press overnight with 5 pounds (1 brick).

5. When the cheese forms a single firm block (12 to 18 hours) remove from press and hoop and rub 1 teaspoon salt firmly over all surfaces. Place cheese on a cheesecloth-covered rack or board. Repeat the salt rub daily for 3 days, keeping the cheese uncovered and at room temperature.

6. Cure the cheese for 2 weeks at a cool (60° F) temperature — the warmest part of the refrigerator will do. Place sliced apple around the cheese for moisture. If a reddish bacteria appears on the cheese, wash it every 3 days or so with a solution of 4 tablespoons salt to 1 cup water.

7. After the 2-week cure, let the cheese dry for 2 days in the colder part of the refrigerator. If any slime develops, wash in the salt solution. When dry, rub with vegetable oil or dip in paraffin.

8. To cure, wrap tightly in brown wrapping paper and then in foil; store in the vegetable drawer of the refrigerator for 2 to 3 months.

Cheddar Cheese

There are very likely as many processes for making cheddar cheese as there are varieties of cheddars on the market. However, almost all cheddar processes are minor variations on a basic method given here. The firm texture and hearty, bitey flavor of cheddar cheese is the product of (1) carefully cooking and firming the curds at a relatively high heat, and (2) at least three month's aging.

This recipe follows the process for Hard Cheese found in the pamphlet which comes with each bottle of Hansen's Rennet Tablets. It is less complicated than most cheddar processes, and yet it makes a superb, hearty cheddar. The color is much paler than commercial cheddars, but that is due merely to the food coloring added by processors. Cheese-coloring tablets, incidentally, are also available from the Hansen Laboratories.

1 gallon whole milk
1 cup buttermilk
¼ rennet tablet
Salt

1. Stir buttermilk and milk together in kettle. In the double-boiler arrangement, bring the mixture to 86° F.

2. Crush and dissolve the ¼ tablet of rennet in 2 tablespoons water. Stir into milk mixture thoroughly — for 1 minute. Let the mixture sit undisturbed at the 86° F until a firm curd develops — 30 to 45 minutes.

3. Test curd firmness with the clean-break test. Then cut the curds into ¾-inch cubes using the method given on page 261.

4. Very gently, stir the curds with long, sweeping movements by hand. Continue for 15 minutes, stirring from the bottom up. Cut up any large, uncut curds that come to the surface. This cures the surfaces of the curds and prevents them from sticking together.

5. Return the kettle to the double-boiler arrangement and heat slowly to 102° F, raising the temperature of the curd and whey about 1½ degrees every five minutes. Stir with a spoon frequently enough to keep the curds from sticking together. Maintain heat until curds hold their shape when held in the hand but fall apart after a few seconds without squeezing. If necessary, the temperature may be taken as high as 104° to firm the curds.

6. Remove the double-boiler arrangement from the heat and let sit for about 1 hour, stirring gently every 10 minutes to prevent the curds from sticking together. Test for doneness by gently squeezing together a small handful of curds. When they fall apart without sticking, you are ready for the next step.

7. Drape a 3-foot-square piece of cheesecloth over a colander and position the colander over a large bowl or kettle to catch the whey. Pour curds and whey into the colander. Then, holding each end of the cheesecloth, roll the curds gently back and forth for 2 to 3 minutes to express all of the whey.

8. Place cloth with curd in a large bowl, sprinkle 1 tablespoon coarse salt over curd and mix well by hand without squeezing. Then sprinkle another 1 tablespoon salt over curd and mix again.

Note: If you are using the coffee-can cheese hoop arrangement, omit Steps 9 and 10 and spoon curd directly into the coffee can. If you use the bandage hoop, you can proceed as follows.

9. Pull the four corners of the cheesecloth together and form curd into a ball. Tie the corners and hang up for about ½ hour to drain whey.

10. Remove the cheesecloth from the ball of curd. Fold a long cloth (torn bedsheet or dish towel) into a bandage about 3 inches wide. Wrap the bandage tightly around the ball, forming it into a round shape. Pin in place and firmly press down to smooth the surface of the cheese. The loaf of cheese, in order to cure properly, should not be more than 6 inches across.

11. Cover top and bottom of cheese with a layer of double-folded cheesecloth. Put the cheese into the press and weight with 10 pounds (2 bricks). Leave for about 8 hours, then turn the cheese over and weight with 20 pounds (4 bricks). Leave in press for about 12 hours.

12. Remove cloths from cheese and let stand on a board for half a day, turning occasionally until surfaces are completely dry. Then dip cheese, a half at a time, in paraffin heated to 210° to 212° F, or rub cheese surfaces with vegetable or mineral oil. Store on a board in a cool place. Turn the cheese daily for several days, then 2 to 3 times a week. This cheese is ready to eat after a month but improves in bite with longer aging.

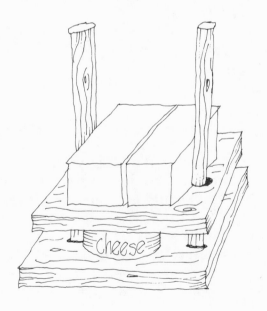

Parmesan Cheese

This is a Parmesan cheese far tangier than the powdered product available on the grocer's shelves. It is fairly simple to make and is well worth doing, considering what an essential cooking ingredient Parmesan cheese is in many households. This cheese may be eaten fresh when soft, but it will gain a spectacularly boisterous flavor when salted, cured and used as a grating cheese.

(*Note:* Although Ricotta cheese can be made from any whey, the cooking process described here conveniently takes the whey through the first step in making Ricotta cheese, page 272.)

5 quarts whole milk
½ rennet tablet
Salt

1. Heat milk to 86° F in double-boiler arrangement.
2. Crush and dissolve rennet in 2 tablespoons cool water and mix thoroughly into the milk. Cover kettle and keep at 86° until the curd shows firm with the clean-break test. This should be about 40 minutes.
3. Cut the curd into ¾-inch cubes, using the method given on page 261. Heat curds and whey as hot as your hands can stand; then press curds into a solid ball. Place the ball of curd in a cheese hoop. Leave the warm whey in the kettle; you will need it later.

4. Press cheese in hoop with 10 pounds (2 bricks) until it takes a fairly firm shape. Turn cheese upside down and press again just long enough to make a firm shape.

5. Set cheese, hoop and all, back into the whey. Heat to just under the boiling point. *Do not boil.*

6. Remove double-boiler arrangement from the heat and allow the cheese to cool to room temperature in the whey.

7. Remove cheese and hoop from the whey and allow to drain in the hoop for 24 hours.

Curing and Aging Parmesan Cheese

Although fresh Parmesan is quite good to eat, it is rather bland. It is best for grating use when aged 4 to 6 months, but it can be used, and does achieve considerable character, after 2 months. The longer Parmesan cheese ages, the sharper it gets.

1. Rub the new cheese well with 2 tablespoons coarse or table salt and store on a shelf in a cool place or in the refrigerator; let dry for 3 to 4 days.

2. When cheese is dry, make a strong salt solution of 1½ pounds of salt dissolved in 2 quarts water. Leave cheese in this brine for 4 days, then remove it, dry the surface and rub with salt again.

3. Store the cheese to dry again in a cool place for 4 to 6 months. Rub gently with salt once a week for the first 3 weeks, turning the cheese each time to dry thoroughly. From then on, continue salting and turning every 3 weeks. If mold appears on the rind, rub it well with salt until the mold disappears.

Ricotta Cheese

Ricotta, a delicate cottage-cheese-like cheese, is made basically from whey and may be used and eaten fresh exactly like cottage cheese. There is absolutely no waste in home cheese making when the whey from other processes is used for Ricotta or in place of water and milk in bread making or other baking.

This recipe is based on the average amount of whey remaining when you have made cheese from 1 gallon of whole milk. The amounts given in parentheses are for preparing Ricotta from 1 gallon of whey.

3 quarts whey
4½ cups whole milk (6 cups)
⅓ cup vinegar (½ cup)
Salt

1. If you are making Ricotta along with Parmesan cheese, simply reheat the whey as soon as the ball of cooked cheese goes into the hoop (after Step 6 in the Parmesan process). Or you may use whey frozen from other cheese-making sessions.

2. Heat the whey until a light layer of cream floats to the surface, then stir in the whole milk and continue heating until just under the boiling point. *Do not boil.*

3. Remove from heat and let stand until a curd forms. As soon as curd rises and pulls away from the sides of the kettle, stir in the vinegar.

4. With a slotted spoon, skim off the curds when they rise again and put in a cheesecloth-lined colander. Let the cheese drain for about 8 hours.

5. Salt to taste and chill before serving. If you prefer, dress with 2 tablespoons whole milk or sweet or sour cream before serving.

The Winter Garden

Glorious Trash

The folks who put out that invaluable gardener's bible, *Organic Gardening Magazine,* have, God bless 'em, an almost messianic vision of compost. Invariably, each issue will contain a shouting compost title like "Garden Your Way to Success with Compost!" or "Compost: Gold in Your Backyard!" When *I* try to talk about composting I always feel a little like the obsessed Ancient Mariner seizing the reluctant Wedding Guest by the arm. Sometimes, though, I can't resist: That dark, rich crumbly soil that compost becomes produces such fat carrots, such bulging radishes, such plump potatoes . . .

As a gardener, I have always been serious about composting, recycling organic materials back into the soil. It is a way of living in partnership with the natural bacterial processes of the earth, and it makes much more sense to me than having my kitchen and garden wastes trucked off — at considerable expense — to be buried in a landfill somewhere. I refuse to be drawn into the seemingly endless argument about the superiority of compost over commercially prepared fertilizers, but I do know compost does wonders for the friability, the desired fluffy texture, of garden soil. Whenever I travel, I yearn to cart home for mulch and compost the abandoned, rotted haystacks in fields, the piles of shredded weeds left along the roadway by the Highway Department, the steaming mounds of manure standing outside horse stables and dairy barns.

Composting is a simple process. Given heat and moisture, most organic materials will break down through aerobic bacterial and fermentation processes and will return minerals and nitrogen-rich humus to impoverished soils. The most direct way to compost is the one my father used: He simply kept a spade in the garden and buried kitchen wastes down a row as they accumulated. Anything from the kitchen except meat scraps and fat can go directly into the garden.

All garden wastes, dead vines, cornstalks, weeds, grass clippings, and so forth, make excellent compost. Simply chop up yard, lawn and garden wastes, let them accumulate in a pile, and then construct a fall or winter compost heap that will work through the rains, freezes and snows of winter to produce a crumbly, soft compost for the spring garden.

The Compost Pile

There are just about as many compost recipes as there are garden composters, but this direct method is the most widely used.

First, find some way to shred or chop the large masses of wastes such as piles of leaves, cornstalks, zinnia and aster plants, pea vines and pole bean vines. Efficient, engine-powered shredders are available but are quite expensive. You can shred piles of leaves by running a rotary lawn mower back and forth over them. I use a corn knife to chop coarse material for compost. A corn knife is one of those simple, sturdy gardening–farming implements no serious gardener should be without. Squared off on the end, it looks like a blunt machete; it was originally used to cut field corn for shocking and to chop green corn for feeding cattle. With a corn knife and a large, round chunk of wood as a block, you can reduce anything in your garden to six-inch compostable chunks in short order.

For the pile itself, dig a pit six inches deep and about four feet by eight feet in size. Then begin building the pile in layers, following this order: first, a six-inch layer of waste — kitchen scraps, garden and yard materials. Over this sprinkle a thin layer of either lime, dried dogfood, rotted manure or "compost powder" — all nitrogen-rich materials which nourish bacterial action that breaks down vegetable matter. Over this spread a two-inch layer of the soil dug from the shallow pit — or any topsoil. Repeat the layers, making the pit as high as you want, always topping it off with soil. Try to slope the pile inwards towards the center to ensure that rainwater will collect and percolate through the compost. Thoroughly wet each layer as you add it. By spring, the pile will be soft, crumbly, earthworm-rich, mineral-and-nitrogen-rich humus, ready for the garden.

Winter Dreams of Summer Greens

As soon as the Christmas mail rush is over, the brightly colored spring seed catalogs begin to arrive, rekindling hope and that stubbornly imperishable dream: the absolutely perfect summer-long garden. This is the year we will beat the accursed powder mildew that sent healthy, full-bloomed zinnias, dahlias and cucumbers into a shriveled swoon. This time the English peas will not turn to lush, six-foot vines, bereft of pods. This year we will cut back on the obscenely prolific zucchini and double up on the fat Fordhook lima beans, which the family consumed before any could be frozen.

The seed catalogs provide as fine a way as I know to offset the earth-born gardener's shut-in winter glooms. My favorites (for sheer enjoyment as well as valuable information) are the catalogs from Henry Field, of Shenandoah, Iowa, and R. H. Shumway, of Rockford, Illinois (called the Seedsman). The big Shumway catalog (11 by 13 inches) is a visual delight and, quite unintentionally, a veritable history of American gardening and farming. (Shumway, which also offers bulk and wholesale feed lots for farmers, has rarely abandoned a traditional seed variety.)

On the cover there's a picture of R. H. Shumway himself, looking like the benign half of the Smith Brothers, taken about 100 years ago. "Pioneer American Seedsman," the legend reads. Inside, there are many color photos (rosy, gargantuan tomatoes, oversized zinnias) and engravings, some of which appeared in the earliest Shumway catalogs 110 years ago. There are pictures of the Shumway and Condon families representing "5 Generations of Seedsmen and Nurserymen," all the way down to Michael F. Condon, age seven. White-haired Grandmother Shumway also appears next to a drawing of a farm cottage in the West, the surrounding plot of earth aswarm with blooming hollyhocks, zinnias, pansies, poppies, snapdragons, salvia, ageratum, alyssum and so on. "For $1," she offers, "you get seed really worth $2 a packet. . . . I will send you enough seed to plant a big bed in your backyard or along your roadside, giving you a gorgeous display all summer long."

There is a sturdy, traditional American life style reflected in these catalogs, the imperishable, though perhaps ever-receding, dream of a small plot of land, peace and self-sufficiency. The Shumway, Henry Field and Burpee seed catalogs tell us how and when to plant, how to cultivate, fertilize and prune and even how to pick and prepare our garden sass. (*Garden Sass* is anything other than field crops such as potatoes, pumpkins, squash and dried beans. A *truck* garden is for the bigger, robust plants; a *kitchen* garden is for the more perishable greens. A *mess* of anything is enough for one meal, such as "a mess of black-eyed peas.")

And then there is the earthy poetry of the
seed-catalog names: among beans, Shumway lists Striped
Creaseback, White Creaseback, Speckled Cut Short or Corn
Hill, Speckled Cranberry and Half-Runner White. Down
South, folks grow a plethora of "field peas" (really beans)
known as Crowder Peas, Purple-Hull Peas and
Whippoorwill Peas. Shumway also lists Six Shooter,
Howling Mob and Shoe Peg corn, truly names to conjure
with. And along with our corn we may plant Potiron,
Jonathan, Tennessee Sweet Potato or Green Striped
Cushaw pumpkins. "Pumpkins for Pies, Canning and
Stock!" Shumway says across the top of the page, "Plant a
Big Batch!"

With pleasure! The seed catalogs remind us that the
earth is rich with possibilities. All that's wanted is our
imagination and toil. Curled up in an armchair with a hot
drink, a gray two-day drizzle carrying on outside, these
winter dreams bursting to be made real recall to us that we
are indeed creatures of the seasons, of this turning world.
Spring is coming, and again it will release our energies into
the garden, into the gathering, cooking and good eating, the
successes and failures, the hard work and laughter of
another year.

Additional Resources

Anderson, Stanley F., with Hull, Raymond. *The Advanced Winemaker's Practical Guide.* New York: Hawthorne Books, 1975. The best next step for the home winemaker who wishes to go beyond the recipes and methods in this book.

Borella, Anne. *Home Canning and Preserving.* New York: Cornerstone Library (Simon and Schuster), 1974.

Bravery, H. E. *Home Brewing Without Failures.* New York: Grammercy Publishing Co., 1965. Considered the definitive book in the field but with a definitely British emphasis on low-carbonated ales and stouts.

Brown, Dale. *American Cooking: The Northwest.* New York: Time-Life Books, 1970.

Eckhard, Fred, and McCallum, Jack. *A Treatise on Lager Beers.* Portland, Oreg.: Hobby Winemaker (2755 N.E. Broadway, 97232), 1970. A thorough demonstration of the difference between British ales and continental European lager beers. Excellent lager beer recipes.

Firth, Grace. *Stillroom Cookery.* McLean, Va.: EPM Publications, 1977. A compilation of country cookery lore on cheesemaking, preserving and storing foods.

Gibbons, Euell. *Stalking the Blue-Eyed Scallop*. New York: David McKay, 1964.

Hansen's Laboratory, Inc., 9015 Maple St., Milwaukee, Wis. 53214. Apparently the sole American source of cheese rennet and natural colorings. They will fill written orders. The rennet package, available in many drugstores, contains a useful set of explicit cheesemaking instructions.

Organic Gardening Magazine, Emmaus, Pa., 33 E. Minor St., 18049.

Rodale, Robert, ed. *The Basic Book of Organic Gardening*. New York: Organic Gardening/Ballantine Books, 1971. The best inexpensive paperback gardening guide.

Seranne, Anne. *The Complete Book of Home Preserving*. New York: Doubleday & Co., 1955.

Sunset New Western Garden Book. Menlo Park, Calif.: Lane Books, 1979. This brand-new revision of an earlier work has been expanded to include regional planting instructions for Montana, Wyoming, Colorado and New Mexico — in addition to California and the Pacific Northwest. An encyclopedic work.

Sweet, Murial. *Common Edible and Useful Plants of the West*. Healdsburg, Calif.: Naturegraph Co., 1962.

Tatum, Billy-Joe. *Wild Foods Cookbook and Field Guide*. New York: Workman Publishing Co., 1976.